# Pets and the Afterlife

## Rob Gutro

## COVER PHOTO

The cover photo is of my first dog, Buzz Wyatt, a Weimaraner puppy that passed on February 22, 2005. The ghosted image was provided by my close friend and fellow dog lover, Lynn Jenner, to whom I am forever grateful.

The experiences in this book are true. However, some names have been altered or abbreviated to protect the privacy of the individual providing the story.

"Pets and the Afterlife: Messages from Beyond," by Rob Gutro. ISBN-13: 978-1497378612 and ISBN-10: 1497378613.

# DEDICATION

This book is dedicated to grieving pet owners coping with the loss of a beloved pet. The physical form of our pets in this life is inconsequential. Pets of all types are members of our family, and dealing with their loss is very real and a significant life event.

I dedicate this book to all of the individuals that work with animal rescues, in kennels, shelters, and in veterinarian medicine who have dedicated their lives to the care and wellbeing of these innocent creatures of unconditional love.

The book is also dedicated to my mother who passed on December 29, 2013 when I was writing this book. She so loved her poodle and cocker spaniel and was so excited that I was writing this book.

Finally, I dedicate this book to our dogs Sprite and Buzz Wyatt whose demonstration of unconditional love provided the inspiration for this book and provided the impetus for me to help those left behind cope with their grief.

# CONTENTS

# FOREWORD

I love dogs. From my work over the years with various dog rescues and charities, I have collected an equal number of "dog" tee shirts and "superhero" tee shirts; the latter attributable to my insatiable love of comic books. I would like to say that I possess the ability to love unconditionally, but this is something that humans develop and learn over a lifetime. Dogs, on the other hand, possess this character trait right from birth; just one of the many reasons I love them.

Since I was a teenager I have had the ability to see, sense, and communicate with those who have passed from the physical world. I have written two other books about my experiences as a way to provide comfort and hope to those left behind; my aim for the books was to help others see that our loved ones who have passed are still with us and come to visit from time to time. But this is my first book devoted entirely to my experiences communicating with animals that have passed, and more specifically – pets.

I hope that by reading this book, you will come to realize that your beloved pet is still around you, and that you will begin to develop for yourself the ability to recognize signs of their presence and reinforcement of their unconditional love for you.

Many of the experiences you will read in this book are my own; others have been shared with the gracious permission of the grieving pet owners to demonstrate how their pets have communicated with them in from the afterlife.

For many decades I ignored my inherited abilities and never paid much attention to them because I lacked the understanding of how to fully use them, and the emotional and spiritual maturity to develop them. As my life started coming together, I fell in love, married, and settled into a reasonably comfortable life with my partner. It was about this time that my abilities began to increase exponentially and became too intense to ignore. The time was right to learn more about this gift that I had received; specifically how to develop the ability to communicate with those who have passed.

As my ability has developed, I have learned that being able to communicate with those in the afterlife is not just limited to communication with humans, but also with animals. I will provide evidence of this later, but I ask that as you read this book, keep an open mind to the things you may not immediately understand; realize that our souls are living energy and that we are all connected both here in the physical realm and in the spiritual realm.

I am not a medium that charges a fee for readings because I am still learning how to develop my abilities. If you would like a personal reading from a more learned medium, I recommend Barb Mallon at www.barbmallon.com, and Ruthie Larkin at Beantownmedium.com. I am available, however, for lectures and speaking engagements. If interested, please contact me through email or my blog.

If you have questions or stories that you would like to share, please write to me at Rgutro@gmail.com, or on my blog: http://ghostsandspiritsinsights.blogspot.com/; Facebook page: https://www.facebook.com/ghostsandspirits.insightsfromamedium or Twitter: https://twitter.com/GhostMediumBook

I look forward to hearing from you.

Rob Gutro

# INTRODUCTION

---

Like many people, I grew up in a family that owned dogs. The first dog I can remember was a copper-colored Cocker Spaniel named "Penny." I believe that Penny laid the foundation for my lifelong affinity for dogs. My mother said that Penny was well-behaved and very easy going. My memories of Penny are few, consisting of only mental images of her walking around in my parents' house, and this one.

I was just four years old in 1967. My mother was talking on the phone that hung on the wall in our kitchen. Dad had taken Penny to the vet earlier that day, and my mother listened quietly to the prognosis. She slowly sank down to sit on the bench. Penny would not be coming home. My mother hung up the phone and wept uncontrollably. One of the earliest memories I can recall is the loss of our family's beloved pet. So many of us have memories just like this, which is why I offer hope and evidence that our pets in the afterlife are capable of communicating with us.

People and animals in the afterlife have the ability to convey messages to the living.

Being a dog-owner, I will tend to focus more on my experiences and interactions that have involved canines; but cats, horses, chimpanzees, and birds all communicate in much the same way. In Chapter 4, I will explain about the intelligence of dogs in an effort to demonstrate their ability to communicate with us. In later chapters, I will share personal experiences that I have had with our own dogs – Buzz Wyatt and Sprite – who, from the other side, have turned out to be two of the best canine communicators in Spirit you can imagine.

Part of this book includes stories submitted by friends and acquaintances. All of these accounts are true. They hold special memories in the minds and hearts of those willing to share them. The intent in sharing these stories is so that others may come to believe there's more to this world than meets the eye.

Through relating these experiences, you will be better equipped to know what signs to look for from your own beloved pets and be able to recognize their attempts to communicate with you.

# CHAPTER 1: LOSING YOUR BEST FRIEND

---

The results of a recent poll suggest that the loss of a pet can be just as devastating as the loss of a family member, and equally as difficult to overcome.

As pet owners, we may be called upon to make that ultimate and final decision in our care for them; one that we will forever question. Did we do the right thing? Would they have recovered if we had just waited a little longer? And we balance this decision against the risk of perhaps waiting too long and causing our beloved pet to needlessly suffer.

We had to make such a decision in 2013 for our dog, Sprite. After his passing, I spent weeks questioning the decision we had made until I began to receive messages from him.

Although the passage of time makes it easier to cope with the loss of a pet, we will surely never forget them. For many of us, pets are our children, and as such, an integral part of our family. In return for unconditional love, they only require our love, attention, and care.

In 2013, while on vacation, my friends Rebecca and Jeff's little black and tan dachshund Eddie escaped his caretaker and was hit by a car. As Eddie lay in the hospital the vets said he would not recover, so his mom and dad had to make the unselfish choice of letting him cross over.

As I was finishing this book in March 2014, Eddie inspired me to call his parents at 9 p.m. to ask if I could include his photo in this book, so his mom and dad would always remember how much he loves them. In fact, he also inspired his parents to give another dog a very happy home and helped them choose the right one.

**(Eddie was always running and doing something! Credit: R.A.E.)**

The following are just a few examples of this exchange between pets and humans.

Pets are very astute and capable of comprehending human emotions such as happiness and anger. With dogs, their understanding of happiness is evidenced by wagging their tails; likewise, anger is understood by laying their ears back or tucking their tails between their hind legs.

As an outward manifestation to others of how much pet owners love and dote on their pets, humans will impose totally unnecessary behaviors on their pets, such as dressing them up in clothing or taking them for walks in baby strollers.

Pets are capable of understanding human language. For example, our dogs smile and vigorously wag their tails when we say the word "treat," and they are capable of name recognition. I love the excitement that dogs evidence when you ask if they want to go for a walk. Whenever I say the word "walk" in the presence of our dogs, the youngest dachshund starts running around and jumping, and it takes a while for him to settle down so that I can put on his collar and lead.

My point in relating these stories is to convey this concept that the love we express towards our pets can be compared to the love we express towards a child. Just as a parent may experience the loss of a child, the pain felt over the loss of a pet is equally comparable. If you have lost a pet recently, my empathize with you. The messages that I have received from pets in spirit fill me up with emotion. Often the message is one of expressing their love for their human parents.

**(Best Friends: Madison and Charlie Clark. Cr: A.M.C.)**

What I have learned is the love that we share with them is often the impetus that brings them back to us when they are in spirit.

# CHAPTER 2: WHAT IS A SPIRIT AND A GHOST?

Before we get started with the discussion of how our pets are able to communicate with us as a ghost or spirit, it's important to provide an explanation of how it works with humans that are in Spirit, because they are remarkably similar.

At the point of physical death, the energy that propels this Earth-bound body combines with the soul, memories and personality of the living being (whether human or animal) and does one of two things: departs this Earthly plane and joins the multitude of other energies that run through the universe as a spirit, or stays here on Earth as a ghost.

In the afterlife, energies that have joined the collective "Spirit" (all of the spirits) have successfully made the transition to the next plane of existence; some refer to this next plane as Heaven, Valhalla, Zion, Paradise or Nirvana. Spirits of people and animals have the ability to return to Earth from time to time to pass messages to the living.

Ghosts on the other hand are energies that have not left this Earthly plane. A ghost may choose to be Earth-bound for reasons that may include the following: their death was either sudden, like an accident or caused by some violent means; they lack the understanding that their physical body has ceased to function; or perhaps there is some matter of unresolved business that may involve revenge or the need to obtain forgiveness from someone who is still living. Occasionally, some pets will stay behind as ghosts if they don't get help from our relatives on the other side (although they usually do).

**(Rob's puppy Buzz crossed into the light. Credit: R. Gutro)**

Although ghosts may be aware of the other energies that have joined Spirit, it is my belief that they are unable to communicate with them across the divide that separates the two realms. If they could, then our late relatives would quickly bring any pets into the light who have either ignored them or chosen to remain earthbound.

Both entities, however, use energy – both physical and emotional energy – as the conduit to help in their communication with us. Entities that possess very low energy levels are capable of tapping the physical energy from an alternative source, e.g., heat, light, moving water, in an effort to boost their energy levels so they can break through the membrane barrier that separate our two existences to communicate with us.

Emotional energy works in a similar manner as physical energy. A group of people gathered together (e.g., a prayer meeting in a church, a funeral or wake, a wedding or birthday party) can collectively raise the emotional energy level and can easily be tapped by an entity.

Emotional energy can be either negative or positive. Earthbound ghosts however, only energize from negative emotional energy, while spirits become empowered by positive emotional energy. Examples of negative emotional energy include fear, anxiety, nervousness, anger and hatred. On the other hand, examples of positive emotional energy includes love, optimism, faith, hope, and happiness. It is important that we provide the right type of emotional energy – preferably position – when we wish to receive a message from Spirit.

There are two types of hauntings associated with Earth-bound ghosts: "intelligent hauntings" and "residual hauntings." Ghosts participating in an intelligent haunting are capable of independent thought and possess the ability to directly communicate and interact with the living.

Characteristics of an intelligent haunting include objects moving independently of their own accord, noise generation (e.g., footsteps, disembodied voices, EVPs), or even physical manifestations such as full body apparitions. Keep in mind that the apparitions require a substantial amount of energy and are usually indicative of an extremely powerful presence. Residual hauntings are not interactive, but rather the "thumbprint" of emotional energy that has been left behind.

Residual hauntings are characterized by repeated actions or scenes, and can be likened to watching a movie that keeps playing the same scene over and over again, as in a perpetual loop. Ghosts participating in a residual haunting do not possess independent thought, and are incapable of communicating with the living.

Our pets are a living embodiment of unconditional love. They, like people, possess the same type of energy as humans. When they pass, their energy has the same choice to make in the afterlife as humans – to either join the collective universe, or remain Earth-bound as a ghost. Anyone that tells you that our pets do not have a soul is quite simply uninformed. Our pets are waiting to greet us when it is our time to pass. It is not unusual for the ghosts and spirits of pets to linger near their masters. I have seen them, as have many other mediums. Wouldn't the world be a better place if only people would learn to love unconditionally?

# CHAPTER 3: ANIMALS MOVING ON OR STAYING BEHIND

---

At the time of their passing, just as with humans, all animals possess the ability to make the decision to either remain Earth-bound as a ghost or to become Spirit (i.e. Earth-bound ghost or spirit in Heaven).

History is abundantly populated with stories of the ghostly appearances of animals. Various books I've read cite ghostly horses running down streets, or ghostly foxes or wolves walking along a highway only to disappear in seconds.

While it is difficult to discern whether these may be accounts of residual or intelligent hauntings, be assured that the majority of animals cross over and immediately walk into the light to join Spirit.

It seems to be a reasonable assertion that the owner-pet bond can be so strong that a pet will decide to linger, and wait for the time of their master's passing, so they can enter into Spirit together. Any pet that stays behind likely does so out of loyalty for their human parents.

When a pet's ghost stays behind, they are typically harmless and not troublesome. However, their presence may cause trouble when new pets are introduced to the home. In the next chapter, I will explain how dogs and cats can sense ghosts and spirits.

**Ghostly Dogs**

In medium Mary Ann Winkowski's book, "When Ghosts Speak," she tells the amazing story about a guide dog that passed and stayed behind as an Earth-bound ghost to continue its watch over his master. When the master adopted another guide dog, the new dog seemingly would not obey the owner's commands. The owner was astute enough to wonder if perhaps her first dog's ghost may still be around. Mary Ann was called in and discovered that the first dog was indeed still lingering in the home. By enlisting the aid of one of the owner's relatives in Spirit, Mary Ann successfully crossed the dog into the light.

**A Ghostly Cat**

My partner and I are active members of a local paranormal group, Inspired Ghost Tracking. During one of our home investigations I encountered the ghost of a pet that decided stayed behind.

The purpose of the investigation was to remove a couple of Earth-bound human ghosts. One of the ghosts was that of a teenage boy. He was a farmhand who had died in the 1800s on a tobacco farm that once existed where the house is today. During the investigation, I felt the tail of a cat brush gently against my right leg. When I looked down, there was no physical presence of a cat where I expected one to be. Absolutely sure of the sensation, I was convinced that it had to be the presence of a ghost cat.

I asked the owner if she had recently lost a cat. She did not, but she had recently adopted two cats. We later learned that the ghost cat was connected to a neighbor, and had joined the two living cats in the owner's house because it was drawn to the feline company.

I have found that whenever it is time for our beloved pets to pass, our loved ones are usually present and waiting for them on the other side to receive them. Conversely, when it is our time to go, our pets will be waiting for us.

**If You Think Your Pet Remains Earth-Bound**

Sometimes, our pets will choose to remain behind as Earth-bound ghosts to stay loyal to their human parents. As with any ghost, they do not belong here and need to cross over. Crossing them over into the light does not mean they can't come back and visit you. Many pet parents have told me how their pets come back from time to time. What's important is that your pets don't linger on Earth as a ghost. Ghosts, whether well intentioned in staying behind to help or care for the living, give off negative energy, and cause negative emotions. They do not belong here and should join the energies of the universe or Heaven.

By the way, ashes do not keep a pet's ghost in the house, but they can act as a draw for the pet's spirit to come back from time to time.

If for some reason you get the feeling that your dog or cat has not crossed over, there are a couple of things you can do. The first thing you can do is call upon one of your relatives who has passed and ask them if they can take your dog or cat's ghost into the light and cross them over.

If you're still feeling that your pet is still with you, then you can envision a white light in a corner of the room. Once you begin to feel the warmth of the light, you can call on a loved one to appear. Then take a treat or a toy that your pet loved during the time they were alive and toss it into the light to get your pet's ghost to cross into it. Your loved one on the other side will help them make that transition.

In later chapters you'll read about dogs who crossed over, but come back in spirit to stay close to their human parents at night. In fact, one dog kept waking up his "mom" every night on a routine schedule, and we know how dogs love routines.

# CHAPTER 4: THE INTELLIGENCE OF PETS

Animals at the time of their passing may choose to remain here on Earth as a ghost or to cross over into the light as a spirit and join "Spirit." The domestication of certain species to be household pets and their constant exposure to humans over time has afforded these animals the opportunity to develop the skills needed to comprehend our language and emotions. Domesticated animals develop the ability to interact and communicate with us during their lifetime; therefore, logic dictates then that they would also be capable of communication with us after their passing. Their messages from Spirit can range from the audible, such as the jingle of a bell attached to a favorite collar, to the physical, such as a cat jumping onto a bed. The discussion in this chapter will use dogs for illustration purposes only; experiences with other animal species will be similar.

Dogs are sentient beings that possess a soul, and are capable of an afterlife existence. I base this opinion on my experiences as a developing medium, a dog parent and my collection of evidence consists of the many messages that I have received from dogs in Spirit that have come to me while counseling their grieving former owners. Mediums Ruthie Larkin, Barb Mallon, Troy

Cline, James Van Praagh, Concetta Bertoldi, and Mary Ann Winkowski have also communicated with pets on the other side.

## Intelligence

University of British Columbia professor, Dr. Stanley Coren is a recognized authority on dog intelligence and behavior. His research shows that dogs possess the intelligence of a 2- to 4-year old child. Dogs have the ability to interpret and process human language and respond to both spoken commands and hand gestures; they likewise can sense human emotions and comprehend when we are upset, injured, or feeling ill. Border Collies, for instance, have been known to understand as many as 1,000 words, a vocabulary that exceeds that of a typical 4-year old child. For more information about Dr. Coren's research, please visit: www.stanleycoren.com.

It is not a tremendous leap in logic that if dogs on the one hand are capable of understanding language and sensing human emotion, then they must also be capable of possessing feelings of their own cognitive volition. Therefore, where anything is possible within the realm of energy, pets in Spirit can communicate with us, the living, using pictures and words that we can associate with and understand.

From my own personal experience observing the intelligence of dogs can be categorized as follows: language and obedience training, game playing, instinctual intelligence, emotional intelligence, routine, location, vocal and body language, facial signals, and other forms of intelligence.

At the end of this chapter, I will share a friend's experience with training her dog. The experience will give you a sense of a dog's ability and desire to learn to communicate.

## Language and Obedience Training

Many pet parents take their dogs to obedience training where they learn good behaviors. Obedience training helps us teach our dogs in several different ways. We teach our dog words or commands that suggest they do specific actions like "sit," "stay," "fetch." Commands also get into language like "go get it," or "bring it back." I've taught our Weimaraner to go check on the other dogs in the backyard, by saying "Dolly, go get Tyler" and she does. Of course some of their favorite words include "treat" and "dinnertime!"

In obedience school dogs also learn hand signals. For the "sit" command I just have to point my index finger down at an angle and our three dogs will sit (except for our oldest Dachshund who loves to show his authority). When I hold my entire hand out, palm facing our dogs, they know to "stay." Two fingers dragged across a small area on the floor means "lay down." When I have no more treats to give the dogs, I hold both of my hands up, open palms facing them and say "no more."

**Game Playing**

Dogs are able to reason. For example, if a dog sees a chipmunk run to an area that has three holes, the dog will check each area. If a dog sees you put one treat under one of four paper cups and you mix them up, the dog will knock over each cup until they find the right one and then may ignore the other. Yes, some dogs can even count!

There are a number of dog intelligence games on the market that will test your dog's ability to reason. Several of them have compartments with a plastic or wooden slider that the dog must push with their nose or paw to reveal a treat.

One such toy we use is the Kyjen 2405 Paw Flapper Scent Puzzle Training Toy. The toy has four flaps that the dog must lift with their nose to uncover the treat below in 8 chambers. The top part of the toy also spins, so the treat can be hidden in a chamber not directly under the flap.

They must learn how to lift treat chambers and rotate the toy to retrieve hidden treats. This toy acts as a scent test and encourages natural searching and foraging instincts.

Our smallest dachshund puts his nose in the compartment and spins it around until he gets a nearby treat. He's also smart enough to look under all of the other flaps. The older dachshund doesn't understand the spinning and just opens the flaps to get the treat directly underneath. Of course, our Weimaraner is so big she can pick it up in her teeth and turn it over, getting most of the treats to fall out. This game is just one of several different kinds that measure another kind of intelligence.

**Instinctual Intelligence**

You can search on the Internet and find countless stories of female dogs who have "mothered" young animals of a different breed, from cats to piglets. Not only is that female dog's instinctual intelligence, but it shows the unconditional love and compassion for all that many humans do not possess.

Dogs also know when someone is hurt and needs help and that can be a human or other animal.

One of the most moving videos I've seen exemplifying this was news footage from a traffic camera mounted over a freeway in Santiago, Chile. One dog was struck by a car while attempting to cross the freeway. Shortly afterward another dog walked onto the highway, dodged traffic and pulled the injured dog to safety from traffic on the side of the road. The video called Hero Dog Saves Wounded Friend was narrated by Sonny Melendrez. It can be found at http://www.sonnyradio.com/herodog.html.

As dog parents know, dogs also understand human health. Your best friend will always be the one who remains close by your side whenever you're not feeling well.

**Emotional Intelligence**

As a dog parent, I have seen our dogs understand and react to our emotions. At times when I'm upset or sad, our dogs will come over and comfort me. If I'm irritated or angry about something, the dogs won't approach me and will let me calm down.

When I'm happy, the dogs will come around, tails wagging and even nudge me to play with them.

Dogs also exhibit jealousy. Jealousy, the feeling of envying someone else for something they have or happening to them, is something that many people thought was a human-only emotion. Dog parents have learned that jealousy is also a dog trait.

Our dachshunds will show jealousy over attention we may be giving to another dog, or may try and take a toy away from another dog.

In the morning, I have playtime with our dogs. That includes getting a number of toys and scattering them on the floor for the dogs to choose their favorite. Then I'll toss a toy or ball, play tug of war or shake a toy.

Often our younger Dachshund and Weimaraner will play with the toys. The older Dachshund, Franklin, usually just stays put until he finally gets jealous enough to come over to me and try to get my attention. In fact, unless I give him my full attention and play only with him, he's not happy.

Whenever the younger Dachshund sees me playing just with Franklin, he'll come over and try to steal Franklin's toy then try to get my attention. They really are just like human children and like children, dogs think about how they're feeling and then they act on it.

Like human children, dogs also pout and feel bad for themselves. Our oldest Dachshund is a known pouter. Sometimes while we're playing with our other dogs, Franklin will sit in a corner and look up at us as if we are ignoring him. He'd rather feel sorry for himself than participate.

## Scientific Proof Dogs Have Emotions

In Oct. 2013, Gregory Berns, a professor of neuroeconomics at Emory University, Atlanta, Georgia, used Magnetic Resonance Imaging or MRI's on dogs to provide scientific proof that dogs have emotions.

MRI's are used to analyze and investigate the body's function in disease and health. An MRI is an imaging technique used in radiology that uses radio waves and strong magnetic fields to create images of the body. Berns' experiment was solely focused on imaging the brain of dogs.

In his book, *How Dogs Love Us: A Neuroscientist and His Adopted Dog Decode the Canine Brain*, Professor Berns spent months training his dogs to practice staying still in an MRI for 60 to 90 seconds. An MRI requires people to hold still while their brain is being scanned. It is difficult for some people to stand still and teaching multiple dogs to do that was an incredible feat in itself.

Berns explained that once a dog was in the MRI and held still, the dog was given commands. Each dog was also shown toys and treats by the dog's owner and by total strangers as the MRI scans mapped the responses in the dog's brains. The MRI results revealed that the dogs reacted much more positively to the owner. That means that the MRI provided scientific proof that the dogs had a stronger emotional connection to the owner, and dogs have emotions just like people.

The study also showed the caudate nucleus part of a dog's brain was active when people who were known to dogs interacted with them. The caudate is the same area of the brain that humans use during anticipation of food, money and love. The caudate is located between the brainstem and the cerebral cortex (outer structured layer of nerve tissue in the brain) and is rich in dopamine receptors.

It's important to know that dopamine receptors are involved in a number of neurological processes, like pleasure, memory, learning, motivation, motor control and more. If you're interested in knowing more, feel free to reference Professor Berns' book. For the sake of simplicity, I'll leave it at that.

Berns concluded that dogs have a level of feeling, including love that is comparable to a human child.

## Scientific Proof That Dogs Understand Emotions

Another study using dogs in MRIs was conducted in Hungary to determine if dogs understand human emotion and the results were positive.

The study was led by lead author Attila Andics, from the Comparative Ethology Research Group at the Hungarian Academy of Sciences and it was published in February, 2014 in the journal Current Biology.

The study exposed dogs to 200 different sounds. Those sounds included noises made by other dogs and people with the exception of spoken language. Other sounds such as mechanical or environmental sounds were played for the dogs to monitor for emotional recognition.

The study focused on reactions in the brain, specifically the temporal lobe and temporal pole. According to Rice University, the temporal lobe is one of the four major lobes of the cerebral cortex in the brain of mammals and is important for language. The temporal pole is the front end of the temporal lobe.

The function of the brain's temporal lobes include understanding language, keeping visual memories and storing new memories, processing sensory input, and emotions.

Andics and her team learned that the brain's temporal pole, which is the front-most part of the temporal lobe - became activated when both people and dogs heard human voices. The study concluded that a dog's brain reacts to voices like a human brain.

The study also found that when dogs heard emotional sounds, like laughter or crying their brains behaved the same as human brains. During the trials with those noises, an area near the brain's primary auditory cortex lit up in both dogs and humans.

The study provided proof that brains of dogs and humans react to emotions the same way.

**Loyalty**

Pet parents know that dogs can be more loyal to them than most humans. While I was researching this book, I came across a short video of an amazing story of a guide dog who was the epitome of loyalty and saved his blind parent during the Sept. 11, 2001 attack in New York City.

The video called "9/11 Salty and Omar - Dog Saves Blind Man" was produced by Allison Argo and appeared in her film "9/11: Where Were You?" for National Geographic.

Omar, blind from an early age, worked on the seventy-first floor of the World Trade Center when American Airlines flight #11 hit the north tower.

During Omar and Salty's descent down the stairs of the tower during the panicked evacuation of the building, Omar chose to let Salty go because being led down the stairs during the panic was difficult. Salty briefly ran ahead but came back for Omar and safely guided him outside before the collapse of the building. Obviously Salty's loyalty and love for Omar made him return against the wishes of his pet parent. The video is on You Tube at: http://youtu.be/1IFVsD6CaTU

Guiding Eyes for the Blind was the organization that trained Salty, and their website is: http://www.guidingeyes.org/.

Once Salty had been instructed to go ahead of Omar, he did as he was told. However, it became apparent that Salty thought about Omar, and out of love and loyalty disobeyed the order to save his "dad."

## Routine

Domesticated animals prefer a routine. Anyone who has ever had a dog, cat or horse knows they're aware of when feeding time occurs. Some pets even remind us if feeding time has passed. They also know when it's time to get up, time to take a walk, etc.

In addition to learning their routine, they also learn the routines of their pet parents. I can't vouch for birds, but some bird owners may tell you that birds know routine as well.

My friend Kathy in Florida told me that cats are no different than dogs. She said that her cat meets her at her door when she comes home around the same time of day. In the mornings as Kathy gets ready for work, she said her cat will go into the bathroom before she does, anticipating her morning routine. He also knows that when she finishes up and leaves the bathroom then he gets a treat.

Whenever I telework, our three dogs seem to know the time. I swear they secretly taught each other how to tell time! At 3:30 p.m. Monday through Friday, they all leave my side and run downstairs to the door where my partner comes in from work.

## On Schedule Messages from a Dog Who Passed

In July of 2013, I received an email from a woman named Janice, whom I had briefly met earlier in the year at one of Medium Barb Mallon's sessions. Janice explained in her email that her dog Tony had passed away on July 5.

In the following series of emails, you'll read how I received messages from Tony that revealed he liked keeping to a schedule when he visited Janice.

Janice said that brought Tony's ashes home and placed them with his collar and a photo on her nightstand. She said that she felt "unsettled" and very sad. She thought that honoring Tony with the picture and collar "would be good and that Tony's spirit would be a positive presence."

In the same email, Janice mentioned she had been waking up at 2 a.m. every night for a while and thought that the spirits of her parents were visiting to let her know they're still around.

She said that if she doesn't happen to wake at 2 a.m. her Beagle named Sam wakes her.

In my email response, I mentioned that Tony may be trying to let her know that he's okay. I told her that living dogs have the ability to see and sense spirits. Janice informed me that Sam and Tony had been canine companions for 12 years, and she knows Sam misses Tony terribly so it made sense that Tony was trying to communicate to Sam.

Janice was feeling guilt over the decision to put Tony to sleep. I explained how we came to terms with that decision with one of our dogs. I told her to list Tony's his ailments as it may help her see he may have been suffering for a while. Tony's spirit told me that he wanted Janice to do the same thing. I told Janice that it is important to make peace with herself over his passing.

Tony shared with me that he is okay and understands the immense self-less sacrifice that comes from making that decision.

I also told Janice the following in an email:

*Before you go to bed, call Tony from the other side and tell him to rest at the foot of your bed tonight. That's a beautiful boy you have (in the photo). He looks a bit younger on the other side, though. (Dogs, like humans appear to us at the time they were most comfortable in life. People who live into their 90s usually appear a lot younger to mediums).*

*Tony has energy and can stand up without wobbling now. He's "wanting those chicken strips" or chicken meat. He's also giving a happy howl to you.*

*Watch Sam tonight and if Sam gets up, tell him Tony is "right there" and sleeping nearby.*

*The visits you get at 2 a.m. aren't from your human relatives. They're very much from Tony. That's why Sam is awake. He hears another dog. :)*

*Tell Tony that you're glad he's okay, and that he can "go to bed now" and rest. Things should quiet down around 2 p.m. after you talk with him... and he says he wants to make sure you cover Sam with a little blanket at night. He's a happy dog, and although he misses being here physically, now he can see when you go in any room and he doesn't have to get up. :)*

Janice wrote me back the following email in response:

*Thanks for writing back, Rob. I really needed just to talk to someone about all of this! I knew you would understand.*

*The 2 a.m. thing is funny: it used to happen before and I was convinced it was my parents and that Sam could sense their arrival. I realize now that it had become sporadic (not the same time every night, although I continue to sleep poorly and wake several times between bedtime and 2 a.m.) and now it has become regular again at 2 a.m. = Tony. Sam sleeps on the side of the bed always where another human would be, and that is the night stand where I put Tony. Sam is having a little trouble getting on the bed lately, so I will put him up there in his usual spot on the pillow between Tony and me.*

*I'm going to bed shortly and I WILL call for Tony. My 13 year old daughter told me a week ago "Tony can HEAR now!!!" (He had been deaf for about one year). I do believe that human and animal spirits are whole on the other side. They are healthy and whole now, just as Tony can walk and hear and steal people food and not get sick or bleed. He was very sick, Rob, he had become increasingly incontinent over the past month and I had purchased washable doggie diapers and changed him often, carried him outside to do his business, etc. When the legs started failing the vet suspected something neurological which could also explain the incontinence, and when he began bleeding, well, there was nothing to stop that really. I KNOW I made the right decision and I am so thankful that it was just me and Tony alone in the end. I know he thanks me. You did the right thing with Sprite also. I firmly believe that they DO tell us when it's ok and it is time.*

*Thank you SO MUCH, your email tonight means the world to me. Janice*

It was important for Janice to figure out Tony was visiting her and Sam "on schedule."

It was also important that she realized she made the right decision for Tony's sake. I was also really pleased to read that Janice's teenage daughter knew that Tony was whole again on the other side. As Janice said in her email, all of our human or animal family members are whole again and devoid of illnesses as spirits.

## Location

Dogs have a great memory for being in certain places and they have a great sense of direction. Part of that has to do with smell working with their memories of places, and they also remember visual cues.

Whenever we drive to visit my in-laws, our dogs always get up and start whining and barking when we turn into my mother and father-in-laws' neighborhood, even though we'd be four streets away They do the same thing whenever they're in the car and we're returning home, even four of five blocks away from our home.

There are accounts of some dogs being lost far from home and finding their way hundreds of miles back home. It seems like some dogs have their own "built in GPS."

## Barks and Body Language

Dr. Stanley Coren explains in his book "The Intelligence of Dogs" that dogs use different barks and body language to convey messages about their emotion or state of mind.

Everyone knows the difference between a bark and a growl. We wouldn't approach a dog who was growling because they're either frightened or in protective mode. There are short barks, yips, moans, panic barks, single sharp barks and other types of barking a dog does to convey a message about their being or their environment. Dr. Coren's book explains the different types of barks and how to understand what your dog is saying.

Body language really conveys what a dog is feeling. For example, a dog that rolls on their back in the presence of another dog is showing submission. A dog who lowers their front paws and has their tail up is in "let's play" mode. A relaxed dog would have their head up, ears up (if pointed), mouth slightly open, tail relaxed and would have a loose stance. So, body language is a way that dogs communicate with other dogs, other animals or people.

**Facial Signals**

Although you may not see it in all dogs, some dogs have different facial expressions to convey thoughts. As someone who has a Weimaraner, I can tell you that some Weims have the ability to move their eyebrows independently to convey feelings. Sometimes our Weim, Dolly will sit in front of us and raise either one or both eyebrows. We've noticed when she raises one eyebrow, she's listening for our vocal cues to see if we would give her a treat from our dinner plate. When we ask her if she wants something, she tends to raise both eyebrows, expressing happiness. Pay attention to any dogs around you to see if you notice similar behavior.

**Other Forms of Intelligence**

Dr. Coren addresses other kinds of intelligence in his book that I haven't touched upon. Several include what he calls "Kinesthetic intelligence," which is the ability to move and coordinate the body skillfully, as required in agility training. He cites that dogs have Logical-mathematical intelligence, and can actually count.

In the *Intelligence of Dogs*, he related the story of a Labrador Retriever whom went after three fishing lures and when asked to fetch for fourth (that wasn't thrown) the dog refused. There are several other forms of intelligence that Coren cites that provide a comprehensive look into the ways our dogs think.

**Telepathic?**

I do wonder if dogs can just look at each other and telepathically tell each other something. On occasion, one of our dogs will get a treat in one room then walk over to another dog in another room and brush up against them, and the other dog will come to where the treat was given.

## Different Dog Breeds and Intelligence

One of the most interesting things I learned is the trainability and intelligence of dogs vary from breed to breed. In Coren's *Intelligence of Dogs*, he included a list of the top 79 breeds of dogs in terms of obedience and working intelligence. Having both Weimaraners and Dachshunds, I totally agree with Coren's conclusions, as I've found that Weimaraners are more easily trained than our Dachshunds. For the harder to train breeds, it is matter of doing more repetitions.

## A Pet Owner's Experience

Because every dog has their own personality and learns at his/her own speed I thought it important to share my friend Audrey's training experience with her dog who had not grown up in a domestic environment. This is particularly relevant for those of us who have adopted or fostered a rescue dog that may have come from the same background.

Following is Audrey's story (in her own words) about the learning experience of her dog Aspen:

*When we acquired our retired breeder dog at 5 ½ years old, it was clear early on that she behaved very differently than a typical pet who grew up in a human environment. From the beginning, we could see that even when she was confused, confounded, and overwhelmed by her new life living with humans in the suburbs, she was always trying very hard to please.*

*Shortly after adopting her, I decided it was hard enough for her to adjust to life with humans and that I should make the effort to speak her "language." The most successful example was looking away as dogs do at a negative behavior. It took practice to turn my head away while indicating a behavior was not desirable rather than making eye contact – but it worked right away. And conversely, I use eye contact to reinforce desirable behaviors.*

*Sometimes it is unnerving to look up while reading or watching television to see that she has been studying my face for clues about me. Dogs really work very hard at that. And I am always touched to observe that she has her nose within a millimeter of my face while I'm still asleep in the morning – looking for any signs of me being awake before nudging her nose up on the bed for a morning pat.*

*Slowly our retired lady is learning typical pet behaviors. After four years of only the occasional bark of once a year or so, she just recently figured out to bark to tell us she wants to come in from the yard – a huge leap for her. And in the evenings when she scurries close around me, I know she is looking for her evening treat snack. After four years her acclimation is still a work in progress, but the large hurdles are behind us. Now if we can just solve her utter terror of cameras.*

### Aspen's Cat Adventure

*One of my favorite memories is [Aspen's interaction] with cats. The breeder had several cats, so the puppies bred there would be acclimated to living with cats. So to Aspen, cats were great playmates, and she was highly insulted that our neighborhood cats would hiss at her and didn't want to play. One even took a swipe at her nose.*

*On one of our walks, Aspen cautiously approached one cat, which was a cat statue in front of a house. Aspen slowly approached this "cat," and the "cat" obviously didn't move. The look on Aspen's face when she got close enough to sniff this "cat" was priceless. She also once tried to make friends with a Christmas yard decoration. Life in the suburbs with fake animals was one of her learning curves!*

# CHAPTER 5: HOW DO PETS TELL US THEY'RE AROUND?

The most important thing I've learned as a medium, is that there is no such thing as coincidence. Understanding that is the key to recognizing your pet's communications from the afterlife.

Often, we immediately attribute things as a coincidence when they're actually signs from Spirit. For example, a spirit can influence you to think about a song that reminds you of them. Then when you turn on the radio the song is playing. That's not a coincidence. That's a signal that a spirit is with you.

When my puppy Buzz Wyatt was tragically killed by a car in front of me during a dog walk on Feb. 22, 2005 I can say that it was the most emotionally traumatic event of my life. I know that may sound odd since I've lost all of my parents, grandparents, all of my aunts and uncles, save one. When my dad passed away three years after my puppy, it was easier for me to deal with his passing because of all of the signs that Buzz provided.

Buzz's strong urge to communicate also fueled my desire to write my first book "Ghosts and Spirits: Insights from a Medium." It was in that book that I conveyed most of the signs from Buzz, but will summarize them here to help you understand ways to recognize signs from our beloved pets.

*(Buzz Wyatt in February 2005. Credit: R. Gutro)*

Spirits of pets do not just communicate directly to their pet parents. The same goes for spirits whom are trying to convey a message to a loved one that refuses to acknowledge signs. Like spirits of humans, pets can convey a message to friends, relatives or strangers whom they know will understand what they're trying to convey, and whom they know will share the messages with the intended recipient.

In the later chapter about my dog Sprite, you'll read about several people who received messages from my late dog Sprite. While I was dealing with grief over losing Sprite in the physical world, he got through to others with messages that he was okay, knowing they would convey the information to me.

It's important not to get frustrated that you're not getting a message after a pet passes. That's because grief always blocks out messages from our loved ones. Sometimes the grief is so intense that it puts up a wall and messages cannot get through.

If you find yourself beyond all comfort, one way you may be able to get a sign is to ask your pet to come to you in your dreams. Spirits who have crossed have that ability.

Before you go to bed, put a piece of paper and pen on your nightstand and talk to your pet - either aloud or in your thoughts. Both voice and thoughts are energy and can be "read" by a spirit.

## Can They Speak in Our Language?

Pets who have passed can communicate in the language they learned when they were alive in physical bodies. As I explained in the previous chapter, pets learn language, understand emotions, behavior, and recognize things.

Border Collies have been known to memorize more than 1,000 words, and your own dog or cat very likely also has a large vocabulary. Although some cat owners have told me in jest that cats don't understand what they're saying so they can purposely not be bothered!

**Ways Spirit Dogs and Cats Can Communicate With Us**

There are many ways in which dogs (and cats) in Spirit can communicate with the living. They include: Appearances that include: doppelgangers, similar animals, or they visibly appear as themselves. They can also give you signs using butterflies, pennies, their favorite treats, or flowers. They can come through to mediums. They can move things, give musical signs, make noises or give premonitions. They can come through with messages in the practice of Reiki, make temperature changes, touch you and even speak in words (bark, meow) to you audibly, telepathically or in a dream.

Whenever a dog or cat communicates with me I can "see" what the pet looks like in my mind. I've seen dogs and cats with very specific markings, like a patch of white on a chest of black fur.

**Appearances: Doppelgangers, Similar Animals, Visible**

**Appearances: Doppelgangers: Animals That Resemble Your Pet**

In Sept. 2013 during an appearance at the Baltimore Book Festival in Maryland a woman named Stephanie asked me about pets and communications. I explained to her that any pet who understands our language or has lived with us in the same environment can be successful in communicating messages to us.

One way that human and animal spirits can let us know that they're around is by influencing us to be in a certain place where we will see someone who looks like the spirit - a doppelganger.

*A Doppelganger Kitty*

Stephanie told me that she had a Maine Coon cat that she loved very much. During her distress over her cat's death she received an amazing sign in the form of a doppelganger.

Stephanie said she worked in a one story building and was looking outside one evening when she noticed a cat on the fence behind the building. She found herself staring at the cat because it looked exactly like her cat. She had never seen that cat until after her cat passed. She sensed that the cat on the fence was a sign from her cat telling her that he was okay and that he'll be around her from time to time.

Once she saw the cat, she felt a sense of peace. Peace is what spirits want for us and that's why they give us messages. After that night the cat never returned. That confirmed that her Maine Coon cat was telling her he was indeed fine on the other side.

## A Doppelganger Dog

Spirits can give messages to people whom they know will convey them to the intended recipient. Spirits don't always have to give messages directly to the person for which they are intended, because that person may dismiss them. So, they have to find someone who would understand the message and pass it on. That's what happened with a friend of mine in New England.

My late dog Buzz was very clever with his message to my friend Lisa. What was really amazing was the closeness in the names of both the dog and the owner to Buzz's name and my name. There is no such thing as a coincidence. It means that Spirit is working to orchestrate the event.

In 2006, when Lisa was out jogging one morning a Weimaraner (same breed as Buzz) came out of a wooded area ahead of her and ran up to her with his tail wagging. She said the dog suddenly sat down in front of her, causing her to stop running.

Lisa decided to say hello and greeted the dog, only to receive a "hug" (the dog jumped up) and kisses.

She quickly figured out why this mysterious dog was there and what he was doing when she looked on his collar and his name tag read "Buzzy." She said she instantly remembered my late puppy's name was Buzz.

Even stranger was the owner's name: Rob Gatsby. Same first name as me, and very close last name.

The dog turned and disappeared back into the woods and Lisa said she has never seen the dog again.

Lisa said that she thinks that Buzz's spirit told "Buzzy" to say hello and let me know that he's still around. Lisa had never met Buzz when he was alive but she knew him now.

## Appearances: Similar Animals

A spirit may not be able to find a doppelganger to give you a message, but they can bring you to the same breed of animal to provide a message. That happened to me while I was vacationing in 2011.

Spirits often communicate on birthdays and anniversaries. The anniversaries can mark a wedding, a birth, adoption, passing or other special event. Spirits communicate during those times just as human relatives that live far away would call to wish you a happy birthday.

I vacationed in San Juan, Puerto Rico on February 22, 2011 and felt the urge to walk down a particular street. I realized after turning down the street the "urge" was prompted by the spirit of my dog Buzz because I encountered a dog walker who was walking a Weimaraner (like Buzz).

In my head I heard Buzz tell me that he was the one who pushed me to walk in the direction of the dog walker. Then he said "do you know what today is?" It was the six year anniversary of his passing and he wanted to ensure that I knew he was still around! So, pay attention to birthdays and anniversaries.

**Appearances: Visible**

It's rare to visibly see an apparition of a spirit, but it does happen occasionally.

Almost three years after Buzz's passing I saw him in full-body form. By that time I had adopted another Weimaraner named Dolly. I was cleaning the kitchen counter and didn't know where Dolly had gone to lay down when I heard a dog's nails on a hardwood floor in the adjacent dining room. I looked into the room and saw the back end of a Weimaraner walking out of the room and down the hallway. So, I called "Dolly!"

There was no response, so I followed the dog down the hallway into the dark living room. When I got there, there was no dog. There were two ways out of the living room. One way was through the closed doors that went into the galley kitchen so I knew she couldn't have gone that way. The other was the hallway where I had just followed the dog into the living room. I was puzzled.

I called Dolly by name and she didn't come. There was no one in the small living room. I started to realize what had happened and went upstairs to find Dolly sleeping soundly, curled up in the middle of my bed! I suddenly realized that dog I saw and heard downstairs was Buzz!

When my dad passed in 2008, I saw Buzz next to my two childhood dogs all waiting in the light for my dad to cross over.

### The First Visible Appearance of Quinn

On January, 2011 my friend Jill emailed me about her beloved dog Quinn's first appearance in spirit:

*Hi Rob - A weird thing happened last night. About 12:30 a.m. I got up from my daughter's bed to go to my room. As I was walking toward the foot of my bed there was a hazy image of my [late] dog, Quinn, lying on the floor. He never slept in my room, always between our doors in the hall. I tried walking around him, as he rolled to get out of my way. I could have been imagining it, as I was half asleep. But it seemed so real, I got into bed and my heart was racing and I couldn't stop thinking about it. Because I'm missing him is my mind playing tricks on me? Very bizarre. I just laid there thinking, I have to ask you!*

My reply:   *Hi Jill - Not weird at all. Quinn was likely there. He knows that you're still grieving a lot and wanted to give you a*

(Quinn smiles for the camera. Credit: Jill D.)

*sign that he's still around you. My puppy Buzz did that, too. He just wants you to know that you don't need to hurt so much, because he's still in the house with you. What a cool story. I love hearing stories about dogs and cats making appearances. It happens a lot more often than you think. Take comfort in it and talk to him this weekend when you're home. He can hear you. Our pets can make a reappearance in physical form, although it's rare.*

### Quinn Influences Sketch, Suggests Contact, Appears

Spirits can do a lot of things. Quinn's next activity included influencing his human sister to sketch him and influencing me to email his mom about him.

On May 22, 2012, Jill's dog Quinn came into my mind and nudged me to I stop what I was doing and email Jill about him (I've never met Jill or Quinn in person).

Jill wrote me back and said: *I swear you are psychic! (Laugh!) How odd you ask! I swear to you, LAST night {my daughter] Heather was sketching him and Milo (their current dog). She'd done about 5 sketches of Milo, and then started one of Quinn. She got his muzzle, eyes and ears very well, then faded out on the body. I was thinking while looking at it how that's how he looked (Quinn's spirit) when I saw him in the bedroom floor--clear but hazy. I told her to fill in more dark on his body 'cause it kinda spooked me.*

## Butterflies and Pennies

Butterflies and pennies are two of the simplest ways a spirit can tell us that they're around us. Often whenever a loved one passes, the living relatives or friends left behind may find pennies or other change. Spirits can drop them in front of you when you're not paying attention. If you do find change, look at the year on the coin. Often the year will have some significance to the loved one who passed or to you or another family member or friend.

My dad, who is in Spirit has been leaving me change since he passed in 2008. I know that because many of the coins have had the year of his passing on them. My late dog Buzz also sends coins, and they often contain the year he was born or the year he passed.

Butterflies and other insects that appear around us are another sign that spirits are trying to let us know they're around. Sometimes they'll appear as if out of nowhere and will linger. If they do, they're likely being influenced by Spirit to stay with us until we understand who is trying to communicate with us.

In the next chapter, you'll read how Sprite, our late Dachshund used butterflies to convey to us and others who were thinking about him.

## Favorite Treats

Dogs love treats, and that's likely one of the first messages you'll get, especially if you own a Dachshund like I do! Spirits have to prove who they are to the living and what better way to do that by talking about their favorite treat.

In my first book I wrote about messages I received from Tegan, a Cocker Spaniel who was euthanized because of a genetic brain disorder that caused her to "go insane." One of the messages from Tegan really stood out. Tegan kept repeating to me the words "chicken or a chicken treat." I assumed Tegan liked them, but didn't understand why that was special and why that message was so loud and clear.

When I contacted Diane with the messages she told me, "the only treats that Tegan got were the freeze dried chicken strips!"

Diane explained that Tegan had a sensitive stomach and other treats didn't agree with her. Diane said "Even though they ridiculously expensive...it's all I really gave her and she loved them!"

**Flowers**

Sometimes our pets will convey their presence through flowers. How would you know if your late pet is trying to get you a message with flowers? Some flowers may bloom where you wouldn't think possible. Or maybe someone you know or don't know will give you a flower or flowers for some reason (the reason is that they're likely influenced by your pet). Flowers need not be living flowers either. They could be plastic flowers or a photo or painting of a flower that may remind you of your pet.

In one instance, a friend's Boxer sent the most amazing floral symbol of love from the other side. I wrote the entire story in my book *Ghosts and Spirits*, but felt it important to cite here because of the power of the event.

My friend Craig's Boxer named Oprah passed on June 26, 2008. Craig said, "Oprah became everything to me: My companion, friend and child. She had the best life and was spoiled rotten with comfort and affection. She also had the best medical care at Anne Arundel Veterinary Hospital for many years. The staff there and at the Target Pharmacy knew me well because of a dog named Oprah."

At 11, Oprah was diagnosed with Cushing's disease and appeared to age quickly. When Craig learned she had internal bleeding that couldn't be stopped he made the ultimate decision. He said, "So yesterday I held my dog, my face to hers, made soft clicking noises and the shot was administered. She died peacefully and will now be cremated."

Oprah's first floral sign to Craig came when flowers bloomed on a bush that had never bloomed before outside of Craig's house. The second sign was much more pointed and powerful. On July fourth,

Craig wrote, "This morning, that bush that never bloomed until Oprah died has now produced a heart. I cut it and stuck it in a vase."

There is no such thing as a coincidence. These "coincidences" are actually a result of spirits working around us to make things happen. So, if you're taking a walk and there's a lone flower on the sidewalk, it may be from your beloved cat, dog or horse.

**(The floral heart that Oprah brought Craig. Credit: C.B.)**

## Medium Impressions

Mediums can also get impressions of the dog's appearance and "hear" the pet convey their life experiences. On Sept. 14, 2013, I attended one of Barb Mallon's medium sessions and received a heartwarming message from a dog for his "mom" who was also there.

The dog that came through to me showed me she was black with a patch of white on her chest. She told me to pass this message to her mom: "Thanks, mom. My back legs work now and I'm running now." The dog told me that she visits her mom at home from time to time and said "I love [visiting] home."

When I read this message aloud at the end of the medium session, a woman named Shannon came up to me and told me she understood the message and showed me a photo of her black Cocker Spaniel named Onyx, who had a white patch on her chest.

My friend and medium Barb Mallon has also tuned into a number of dogs and cats. She has provided descriptions of the pets, their habits, favorite things and sometimes their names. In later chapters, you'll read Barb's experiences with her dog in spirit and medium Ruthie Larkin's messages from her dog.

## Movement

It takes a lot of energy for a ghost or spirit to move something. To do so, there has to be a large source of energy that can be tapped. Energy sources that can empower both ghosts and spirits include all physical energies: heat, light, and water. Emotional energy can also power them but only negative emotions like anger and fear provide energy to Earth-bound ghosts while positive emotions like love energize spirits.

One common movement I've learned about from cat owners usually occurs on the person's bed. People who owned cats will sometimes report feeling a cat (when there's none in the house) jump on their beds and curl up at the foot of their bed.

My late dog Buzz was a "mover and shaker." Shortly after Buzz passed he moved a sneaker in front of my former roommate. It was no surprise that he chose a sneaker to move to prove he was still around. Buzz had an affinity for shoes and sneakers because he often mistook them for chew toys!

The night he passed Buzz provided a physical sign of his presence. After the accident I transported his body to the vet and they took him inside so I could say a proper goodbye before he was cremated.

While standing in the vet's parking lot with a couple of other friends who met me there, about 30 feet from where we were all standing, suddenly, a lid popped off a trash can and came crashing on the ground. We looked over and there was no one there. There was no human or animal around and winds were calm. I knew it was Buzz telling me that he was still around, and everyone agreed it was a sign from him.

The lesson here is to be aware of things around your home. If you wonder how something moved from one place another (aside from you forgetting where you left something) it may be that one of your pets in Spirit moved it. Pay close attention to things that they enjoyed. Human spirits often move objects, too!

**Musical Signs**

Spirits commonly use music to let us know they're around. They'll influence us to turn on a radio and when we do a song will be playing that reminds us of them.

My puppy Buzz was a great one to use music to let me know he was around often. The night he was killed and I returned home there were two relevant songs playing on the radio (that was turned on in the house): "The Dance" by Garth Brooks, and "(My heart is empty like a) Monday Morning Church," by Alan Jackson. Both are about love and loss. Those two songs would come up over and over in the course of a couple of years whenever I or someone else I knew was thinking of Buzz, although "the Dance" was already 15 years old and rarely played on the radio. You can find the entire story in my book *Ghosts and Spirits: Insights from a Medium.*

So the next time you get into your car and are thinking about someone who has passed, either human or pet, pay attention to the song on the radio. It may be a message from someone who loves you on the other side.

**Noises**

If you've ever watched ghost hunting television programs, you've noticed that ghosts like to make noises that seem to come from nowhere. Spirits do the same thing. It's almost like energy build up (from the love you have for them) enables them to make a noise to let you know they're around. Some of the most common ways that dogs in Spirit will let you know they're still around include a short bark, the sound of their nails on the floor, snoring, a collar jingle or rustling noises as if playing with a toy. All of those sounds are ways dogs and cats can let you know they're still around or have come back to visit.

A friend of mine had a Dachshund named Rusty who passed at 14 years old. During a visit to a friend's house, as I stood in his hallway I distinctly heard a rustling sound on the floor as if a dog were shaking a toy. Rusty was still around and still playing in his dad's house

Sometimes when I walk by the corner of our hallway where our late dog Sprite used to sleep, I swear I've heard him snoring.

Next time you're home and it's quiet stay still and listen closely. You may still hear your cat, dog or bird trying to communicate with you.

**Premonitions**

One of the strangest experiences I've ever had was a premonition of danger, in a warning I received from Buzz in spirit. If you get feelings of dread, they may be influenced by a spirit who is encouraging you to take extra precautions. Listen to your feelings.

The strange thing about this warning was that it was on the date my new dog was the exact same age of my late dog at the time of his passing.

Wednesday, June 22, 2005, marked four months to the day that Buzz was killed. Buzz was born on July 29, 2004, and died on February 22, 2005. Buzz was 6 months and 23 days old, and the accident occurred around 5 p.m. eastern time. Dolly was born on November 29, exactly four months later than Buzz. On June 22, 2005, she was also 6 months and 23 days old.

Buzz's spirit told me to "watch Dolly's leash." I took that to heart and walked Dolly in a wooded area instead of along the main street, just to be safe.

As we were walking in the woods, the clasp on Dolly's leash mysteriously came open! I was so thankful for Buzz's message that helped protect Dolly by having me take her on a different route.

Buzz knew that exact time in Dolly's life was critical and wanted to ensure she was safe and get past it.

If you get a premonition, it's likely a message that a spirit is trying to convey to get you to act or not to act. To most people it feels like a strong urge, and it's something you should listen to. I listened and likely saved my new dog's life that day.

## Reiki

Reiki is an energy healing method that originated in Japan. Reiki is basically a mediation that enables one to tune into information that is around all of us, such as spiritual or emotional energy. Reiki is based on the idea that an unseen life energy flows through us and is what causes us to be alive. Reiki taps into energy. Spirits and ghosts are energy, so, the meditation provides the ability to connect with them.

When Buzz passed I contacted Fay Fowler Gross, a Reiki healer. She was able to tune into Buzz's spirit energy and provided me with messages that proved she was talking with him. It was very healing to me and I recommend talking with someone learned in Reiki to communicate with your beloved pet.

Because Reiki taps into energy, it is an amazing practice for healing. In 2014 I had Reiki work done on my shoulder and the pain subsided.

## Temperature Changes

Whenever a spirit or ghost appears, there is sometimes a drop in temperature. The scientific reason that happens is because the entity removes the energy of motion from the molecules of air and the molecules slow down.

Air molecules are matter and they need energy to move. When air is heated, the molecules move faster and spread further apart. When the energy is removed, the molecules slow down, condense and the air cools. When that happens, those temperature drops can be recorded on a digital thermometer.

So what does a ghost or spirit do with the energy they absorbed from the moving molecules? They use the energy to empower themselves to convey messages in any number of ways.

When my dad died in 2008, he actually came to me that night and gave me a cold hug in my kitchen. He drew the energy out of the air to allow me to feel his hug.

Three months after my puppy Buzz passed, he also took the energy out of the air molecules and created a "cold spot" to let me know he was present. As I was putting together my other dog's breakfast,

Buzz wanted to make sure that I knew he was there, so he absorbed a lot of energy from the motion of air molecules (spirits are energy after all), and he slowed them down, cooling the air on one side of me. That's when I felt the entire left side of my body grow ice cold! What was odd was that my right side was actually perspiring from the warmth in the house.

I immediately sensed Buzz around, turned to the left, looked toward the floor and called his name out loud. The cold feeling on my left side faded quickly. Buzz had moved and was waiting for his breakfast right under my feet as he did when he was alive!

Buzz's spirit used the same method of communication another time when I was on the floor playing with my dog Dolly. I suddenly felt a cold sensation and weight against my back. I knew it was Buzz because when he was alive I would lay down on the floor to play with him and sometimes he would go around me and lay down against my back.

Buzz wanted to be there for playtime that morning. Just as other pets will come to you for attention when you get on the floor, spirits of pets may also do the same, because it's still playtime to them, even from the other side!

66

**Touch**

Touch is a common way for our pets to communicate with us from the other side. Temperature changes are even a form of "touch."

Don't be surprised if you feel something against your leg where your dog used to put his nose. Or you may feel your cat's tail brush up against your leg.

During a private investigation with the Inspired Ghost Tracking Group when a ghostly cat brushed my leg I asked the homeowner if she's ever heard or felt a cat. She confirmed that she had felt a "ghost" cat jump up on the end of her bed and curl up when there were no cats in her home.

I received an email from a woman named Andrea who told me that her beloved late cat named Barney had been making "return appearances." Barney was Andrea's best friend of 16 years.

She noted that she had Barney's ashes in her bedroom and I told her that ashes can act as something of a magnet to spirit. That doesn't mean that if you have a pet's ashes in the home they'll be around all the time.

What triggered Barney's appearance was Andrea's health. Andrea said that Barney's spirit started coming around when she fell ill proving that a pet's love and compassion doesn't end when they pass. Andrea said that she also felt Barney touch her twice on the leg.

Another email I received about a pet communication came from a man named Mark. Mark thought his dog Patches may have visited him. He said that he was lying in bed one night and he had an experience that a dog was pawing on his hip, but he was alone with the door closed. He said out loud, "If that's you, Patches, I'm glad you're here." Mark said that he can't prove it, but he had a nice feeling at the time. The important thing is that Mark realized that Patches had come to visit and didn't discard the wonderful visit.

**Words: Audibly, Telepathically or in a Dream**

Pets in Spirit can use words in a number of ways to let you know they are present. Mediums tend to hear names, but you don't have to be a medium to hear your pet's name. Spirits of pets can influence you to be near someone who is talking about someone with the same name. In the same manner, spirits can influence someone to turn on the radio at a given time to hear their name.

Dogs and cat spirits are good at communicating their own names to mediums and they do it telepathically. Because they know their own names, they can share them.

While attending one of medium Barb Mallon's sessions in Virginia, I remember her talking about a little scruffy dog named "Peanut" running up and down the main aisle of the room. As it turned out, Peanut belonged to someone in the room who really missed their beloved dog.

One of my favorite messages from a dog involved a small beige-colored Chihuahua that came through to me at one of Barb's later sessions. This dog was quite feisty and energetic. I heard him tell me his name was "Chico." In my mind I asked Chico to whom he belonged.

A couple of minutes passed and a younger woman with long dark hair came toward me on her way to the restroom. Chico told me that was his "person" so I stopped her. When I asked her if she knew "Chico" she was shocked. Chico was her grandmother's late Chihuahua.

So why was Chico there? He told me he was "assisting" the woman's black mid-sized dog how to be a better pet. The woman gasped because she did indeed have a Black Labrador Retriever.

The easiest way for a spirit to convey a message to anyone who is overcome with grief, is for the pet to come into a dream. Spirits use dreams to convey messages because our logical minds are at rest and are emotions are in check. Sleep is a time of calmness that enables a spirit to come through.

Look for any of these kinds of communications from Spirit to give you the comfort and message of hope that you're seeking. Know that our pets are at peace on the other side, and they can work in many ways to let you know. These are not the only signs pets can give, I'm sure there are more. It's all about paying attention to the world around you and not discounting something as a coincidence. There is no such thing as a coincidence: it's Spirit in action.

# CHAPTER 6: SPRITE'S JOURNEY AND AMAZING MESSAGES

---

This chapter addresses a situation that many pet owners either have or will confront, and provides proof of how one very special dog named Sprite communicated the same messages to three different mediums that had never met or communicated with each other.

It's a very personal story about one of our dogs that I hope will provide both proof and comfort that your beloved pet is safely with Spirit, and capable of communicating with you from the other side. It is not uncommon for messages from your pet to be initially blocked because of your grief. In cases such as this, I recommend consulting with a medium, or perhaps even a Master of Reiki.

I am very fortunate to count other mediums among my closest friends and during my time of grieving, all of them contacted me and conveyed very similar messages from our beloved pet that had recently departed.

## When is "the Right Time"?

Every resource I read acknowledged that knowing when to let go of a beloved pet is an extremely intense and deeply personal decision. The tendency to second guess the decision to put down a pet is a normal part of the grieving process; feelings of grief can easily migrate into feelings of guilt. Although it's natural to have these mixed feelings, we need to remind ourselves that our pets cannot tell us when they are experiencing pain and are ready to go.

Such feelings and emotions are exactly what we experienced when making the decision to let go of our dachshund, Sprite, whose quality of life rapidly diminished in a very short period of time.

## Sprite's Story

Sprite came to us as a foster through a local rescue in early December 2010; he was just a few weeks shy of turning 14 years old. Sprite had been turned in to the rescue after his owners, an elderly couple, both passed within months of each other.

**(Sprite in 2011. Credit: R. Gutro)**

When he first came to us, Sprite was not housetrained. And because he had not been to a vet since 2006, he required all of his routine shots to be updated. Other required medical procedures included neutering, the extraction of 22 rotted teeth, and removal of a large tumor-like growth from under his chin.

Sprite was not accustomed to being hugged, and would release a little grunt under his breath when squeezed. He never returned affection, such as giving us "kisses" – which was probably a good thing because of his rancid breath. He never played with toys, nor engaged in tug-of-war or other games with our other dogs. It wasn't until December, 2012, that Sprite finally began to approach me to get a head rub, or greet us when coming in the door.

It was during a routine visit that our vet informed us of Sprite's irregular heartbeat. With that diagnosis, options for treatment of future ailments would be severely limited; for example, he could no longer be anesthetized. She also cautioned that if he were adopted out, that the stress of adapting to yet another new home environment could be potentially fatal. So in mid-2011, we decided to adopt Sprite and expand our brood of canines.

Sprite eventually bonded with our other dogs, and we were a contented three-dog family. But in 2012, Sprite's health began to decline marked by the loss of sight in one eye, and diminished vision in the other. His hearing also declined, and his kidneys began to fail as evidenced by his inability to retain urine. In the first half of 2013, we began to ponder whether Sprite's time with us was rapidly drawing to a close.

On the evening of July 7, around 9:30 p.m., Sprite developed an uncontrollable nose bleed. The bleeding became profuse and would not clot; the flow of blood caused him to sneeze. At 10:30 p.m., his breathing became labored so I took him to the emergency vet's office. Sprite responded to treatment after 30-45 minutes, and the vet successfully managed to control the bleeding.

The new diagnosis, however, was that Sprite had possibly developed a tumor in the nasal cavity. The testing for a tumor required that he be put under. Because of his lengthy list of other ailments, it was at this time the vet asked if I wanted to euthanize him that night. I refused. If Sprite's time to pass was drawing near, I wanted him to be at home with us.

On July 8, 2013, at 5:50 p.m., my partner and I said goodbye to our oldest canine "boy" in the vet's office. He passed peacefully with each of us holding one of his front paws. As the words, "His heart has stopped" were spoken, such a sense of finality was conveyed that the flow of tears could not be stopped. After a few moments alone with him, the vet entered the room and gingerly removed the limp body. And that was the last we saw of our Sprite.

## The Questioning

After euthanizing a pet, the feelings of guilt and tendency to second guess the decision made can be overwhelming. We went through it, too. A couple of days after Sprite passed, I responded to a friend's email by recounting my observations of Sprite's health that led to our decision.

If you are a pet owner, I urge you to do the same. Email a friend, tell them in detail what you have observed, and ask for an impartial opinion. Then read it over and over again. Once I read the email that I sent to our friend, I realized that it had been the right thing to do, and it had been the right time to let Sprite pass. The following is my email to our friend Merle:

*Date: Wed, 10 Jul 2013*
*Hi Merle - We are still questioning if we did the right thing with Sprite. I've gone over this a hundred times already. I'm writing these things down to help us understand that it was best for him.*

- We knew Sprite was failing last year when he couldn't walk around the neighborhood anymore.

- We knew he had a bad heart murmur and his kidney failure really became bad around January, when he had to go out every 5 hours or so, and immediately after he ate and drank.

- I put towels down in the kitchen for him overnight, and I know he felt badly every time he peed in the house.

- Last week, he couldn't even get up and peed on his bed and blanket.

  His little back legs were weak, and for the last 6 months I've had to carry him up and downstairs. In the last couple of months I've had to carry him outside, and sometimes back inside (he couldn't get strength in his back legs and his muscles were wasting).

- Our friend, Yolie let the dogs out this weekend and had to pick him up and bring him outside, too.

- He was blind in one eye, and could only see light and shadows in the other.

- He walked into walls and doors.

- He was going deaf, too.

- Last week he stopped eating his kibble and the wet food. He would only eat treats.

- After Sunday night in the Emergency Room, the vet there said that his 2 1/2 hour nosebleed could be from a tumor and any tests would require putting him out- which would've killed him. She said they stopped the bleeding, but couldn't promise it wouldn't return.

*- He stopped holding his tail up in the air. His tail used to always stay pointed up, and wagged all the time.*

*- Another indicator was when he stopped being engaged, and would wander off and sit facing a wall for hours at a time. It was almost like he had "checked out" on living.*

*Taking into account all of these things, and the lack of interest in dinner (which has never happened), Sprite looked old and tired and worn out. We thought that with the bleeding possibility and everything else, that it was time. I just hope we were right.*

After I sent this email, I read it over and over again, and it really helped me come to terms that we did the right thing at the right time for little Sprite. I recommend that any pet owner evaluate their pet's quality of life, and make a list if you have to, to determine if you're doing the right thing. As difficult as it is, you must also be strong for your beloved pet. Remember, they will be around you - as the next part of this story proves.

\*\*\*\*\*\*\*\*\*\*\*\*\*\*\*\*\*\*\*\*\*\*\*\*\*\*\*\*\*\*\*\*\*\*\*\*\*\*\*\*\*\*\*\*\*\*\*\*

## Sprite's Messages to Other Mediums

On Wednesday, July 10, 2013, I wrote down all of the messages that my friends and fellow mediums Ruthie Larkin (BeantownMedium.com) and Troy C. sent me after our dog Sprite passed away. In addition to these incredible messages from Ruthie and Troy, my friend medium Barb Mallon (Barbmallon.com) called later on July 10 with another incredible confirmation from Lisa, a student in her psychic development program.

These messages were so important to us because our grief was blocking any communication from Sprite on the other side, as grief usually does. What's amazing is that these three mediums confirmed each other without knowing each other, and confirmed some things that we were sensing. We are so blessed with their friendships and their gifts made dealing with Sprite's passing so much easier for us.

So, to the pet owners who go through this, if you doubt yourself, suffer guilt over letting your dog or cat pass out of pain, please consider seeking out a reputable medium. Ruthie Larkin and Barb Mallon both have the abilities to help you.

**Sprite's Messages to Troy**

**Following are the text messages that Troy sent me about his encounter with Sprite:**

*July 9 at 9:40 a.m. EDT:*
*TROY: Excuse me, but Sprite has been running around my house playing this morning like crazy! Even (my cat) Marilyn steps out of the rooms he's in and just stares back at him! LOL. He wants you to know that he can jump like crazy now... which made taking a shower rather interesting this morning.*

*Oh, and one more thing... Apparently he really liked the food dish that he ate out of and wants to make sure that you continue to use it with the other dogs?*

*July 9 at 1:11 p.m. EDT:*
*ROB: OMG... thank you. I was wondering what to do with his special dish. Thanks, Troy. I'm a mess...*

*July 9 at 1:55 p.m. EDT:*
*TROY: He was so happy to have full movement again. You should've seen Marilyn's face! LOL Somehow what to do with the dish was*

*really important to him. Continuing to use it with the other dogs is his way of caring for them.*

*July 9 at 7:48 p.m. EDT:*
*ROB: Thank you, Troy. He has a square ceramic dish that we got special for him because he wouldn't eat out of a bowl. I'm going to use it every night to put our dessert in when we go upstairs to watch TV. It was Sprite's special dish, because the other dogs have bowls. It's amazing. He told you it was a dish and not a bowl. I love you, Troy. You've made both Tom and I feel better - my grief is blocking messages and I needed to hear from Sprite.*

*July 9 at 7:51 p.m. EDT:*
*TROY: Awww... I think Sprite would like that. :) I figured that's why he came to my house! He knew I'd listen and tell you everything! LOL.*

*July 10 at 6:35 a.m. EDT:*
*ROB: Troy, Tom and I are feeling a lot of guilt for bringing Sprite to the vet (and euthanizing him). I know he was really failing, but did you get a sense he was okay with it, and he was tired and ready to go? We're struggling and have questioned ourselves over and over.*

*July 10 at 8:39 a.m. EDT:*

*TROY: Trust me when I say that I have NEVER seen a dog so happy to be free of his failing little body. :) He did nothing by jump and play/tease my cat. I almost called you to see how to make him leave her alone! LOL. It was adorable. The feelings he conveyed were full of love towards you guys and the dogs. :)*

*He is such a little care-taker! Making sure that you continued to use the dish was so important to him. It will give the other dogs a sense that he's still around for them... and you.*

*There was NO sense of sorrow, anger or resentment. Only excitement, relief and love. That tells me that you did the hardest ever, loving thing possible for him the other night. From what I sensed and saw in Sprite yesterday, thankfulness is (what he is conveying).*

*July 10 at 9:18 a.m. EDT:*

*ROB: Thank you, Troy. I'm sitting here all teared up.*

Troy was "told" by Sprite that his "dish" was special. Sprite is the only dog we have that had a flat dish and not a bowl. Sprite could not eat out of a bowl (because he had a hard time seeing into it). Troy didn't know any of this, but Sprite used the dish as proof the message was from him.

**Sprite's Messages to Ruthie**

Medium Ruthie Larkin provided several messages of proof the Sprite was indeed communicating with her and totally shocked us. She pinpointed a special blanket, and identified the three spirits I asked to come into the vet's office with us when it was Sprite's time. There was no way she could know the exact three spirits that I was asking to help me. Further, she confirmed that they were there when I felt them in the vet's office. Here are the messages she received:

*July 10, 2013 2:53 p.m. EDT*
Ruthie called me. She said that Sprite came to her yesterday (same day as Troy) and did the same thing for her that Sprite did for Troy. She started writing this note, and had to call me today at 2:45 p.m. because as she was writing it, Sprite came back in!

*July 10, 2013 14:51:31 -0400*
*From: Ruthie Larkin (www.beantownmedium.com)*
*To: Rob Gutro*
*Subject: HERE'S THE EMAIL WHERE I HAD TO STOP AND CALL YOU*

*Thank you Rob! I know you are grieving for your little Sprite and I appreciate you taking the time to interpret this photo for me. By the way, I thought of Sprite yesterday and when I did I saw him very clearly jumping around and in beautiful shape and very happy. You know I don't always get the pets but he came in very clear. In fact, he is showing me right [this is where she stopped writing]*

\*\*\*\*\*\*\*\*\*\*\*\*\*\*\*\*\*\*\*\*\*\*\*\*\*\*\*\*\*\*\*\*\*\*\*\*\*\*\*\*\*\*\*\*

Ruthie stopped writing and called me and said Sprite was jumping up and down, saying "thank you, thank you." He told her that he was actually in a lot of pain and his stiff legs hurt a lot and now he is finally free of pain. She said that his coat is shiny and bright, and he appears in full health, and is very grateful to us for making the choice.

Ruthie said (and later wrote this to me in an email so I would have it) *"Sprite sent you love through me 3 separate times. When a Spirit wants to send love they will fill every cell in my body with an unbelievable feeling that goes from my toes to the top of my head. You know how you will get chills when you receive confirmation from Spirit... well, this is 100 times better!!! I can barely say a word when it comes through and I always immediately know that my client (in this case Rob) is receiving a great deal of love from their deceased loved one."*

- She asked if he was wrapped in a special blanket, and I told her that we took him to the vet and wrapped him in his favorite dark blanket. Ruthie said that Sprite wants that blanket around. I told her I was planning to put it under his ashes and she said that's perfect.

- She also noted that Buzz (my first dog, who tragically died when his leash opened in Feb. 2005 and was killed by a car) is with him. She said: *"Buzz looks like a smaller dog, though, even though I thought he was a Weimaraner."* I told her that Buzz was a puppy when he passed.

She also validated what my partner Tom said about Ed's spirit. She said that Ed is very happy to be with Sprite (and happy to finally have a dog). The night Sprite passed, Tom said, "I'm sure Ed is happy because he finally has the dog that I didn't let him have." Ruthie then told me that she also saw my Dad around Ed, Buzz and Sprite. She said that my Dad was also with them.

I then told Ruthie that before we walked into the vet's office with Tom and Sprite, I asked Ed, my dad and Buzz to be in the room to help Sprite when he passed. She acknowledged that's why they all came through to her. They were there when Sprite passed. I told her that when Tom and I were alone in the room with Sprite after he was sedated, I felt both of my elbows get cold and sensed Ed on one side of me, my dad on the other, and Buzz sitting on the floor. Ruthie's message confirmed it.

Ruthie asked if there was another "Buzz" that my dad knew. She later wrote me *"when I said that your Dad said there was another meaning to the word Buzz and it did not belong to a dog I meant it was a person. Little did I know that it was YOU!"* I told her that back in 1993 I was given the nickname was "Buzz" by friends in Florida.

Ruthie said that Sprite was the third pet to ever come through to her, and he came through twice in two days. She said that he absolutely does NOT want us to feel guilty. She said that it was courageous to take him out of pain. She said that he was really in a lot of pain, although it may not have been noticeable.

I told Ruthie about Troy's reading and Ruthie contacted him. She told him: *Troy – I've heard so much about you and hope to meet you someday soon! Yes, we were both totally confirming the messages Sprite sent to us.* Ruthie assured me that our precious little Sprite is finally pain free and filled with joy.

## Sprite's Messages to a Developing Medium

When I came home from work on July 10, 2013 I had a message from my friend and medium Barb Mallon. Barb does readings and teaches psychic development classes. She called with a special message from one of her students, whom I met for the first time the previous weekend at one of Barb's medium events.

Lisa is an engineer who has been trying to develop her medium abilities and has taken Barb's courses. Earlier that afternoon (three days after Sprite passed), Lisa had a consult meeting about being mentored with Barb Mallon and if she felt comfortable, it was supposed to be Lisa's first mini reading.

Barb said that because it was going to be Lisa's attempt at a mini-reading: *While driving to my office I asked if any of my people in spirit would like to say hello and/or help Sprite to say hi - to let me know he's okay, so I could pass it along to Rob. I specifically asked for my friend "T" in spirit to help, because he was a huge dog lover.*

Among other things, Lisa told Barb that she had heard a dog barking in spirit for about three days before their meeting. The first day Lisa heard the barking it was July 8 (the day Sprite passed). Barb said: *I perked up immediately knowing that's when Sprite passed.*

Barb Mallon shared the sequence of events on how she and Lisa came to understand that Sprite was communicating to them:

*In the midst of answering questions for Lisa, she asked if it was normal to hear things randomly and bought up that she had been hearing a dog in spirit bark for three days.*

*I asked how the bark sounded and she said, "not frantic, not hurt and it felt like the dog wanted to tell someone something." I offered NO information and simply addressed this by answering that many times, spirit hangs around a few days prior to when a message needs to be delivered.*

*[At the time] Lisa was reading Rob's first book, "Ghosts and Spirits: Insights from a Medium" and the chapter about the passing and messages from his first dog, Buzz, so she knew who Buzz was.*

*At the end of the lesson when we started the mini reading, I asked her to try to tune into the dog she'd heard barking. She immediately got the reference of Buzz and his accident having no idea that the dog I thought she was hearing was [Sprite].*

*While I knew this is NOT how Sprite passed, it felt to me that Buzz was possibly coming in to bring through Sprite, so I acknowledged that, no, this wasn't the same dog and to try to focus on the barking dog more. Again, she had NO idea it was Rob's dog, but I found it interesting that Rob's reference and dog were used to open the circle for Sprite.*

*She was NOT used to giving info in a reading and didn't quite know what to do. Suddenly, she gasped and the info would just hit her. She gasped and "felt" both Rob and his Tom's feelings and Sprite's with the key info she was getting.*

Barb asked Lisa to focus. Lisa said that she saw another dog on a vet's table where he passed. It appeared to be a dog with some white on his muzzle on in his front (Sprite had white on his muzzle and a white patch on his chest). Lisa said the dog was put to sleep on the vet table (Sprite was put to sleep on the vet's table – Buzz died from being hit by a car, so it wasn't Buzz).

Lisa said she saw a red ball and a twisted multi-colored rope around Sprite. Although Sprite never played with toys, he loved to sit in our upstairs room where we have a red ball that lights up (and our other dogs played with it) and rope toys.

Lisa told Barb that the dog's spirit, or Sprite's spirit as it turned out, was "bouncy happy!" Barb said: *Once I knew who it was (Lisa had no idea) I asked if this dog had any MESSAGES for his owners. She felt incredible chills at first and then again gasped.... "BOUNCY HAPPY!!! BOUNCY HAPPY!!! I MEAN REALLLLLY... BOUNCY HAPPY!!!" This made me tear up as I knew Rob and Tom needed to hear this.*

The message was that Sprite was happy and now totally healthy on the other side. That's exactly what Troy and Ruthie Larkin conveyed in their messages from Sprite. This was a triple confirmation from three people who, at the time, didn't even know each other.

Lisa said that Sprite felt "so tired, sleepy, and ready to go." This is exactly what I thought Sprite was feeling the day we took him in for his final vet visit, and this was so comforting to hear.

Barb said: *I believe Sprite connected to her well because she does not have human children and her fur babies are her children, so she gets it.*

Barb wrote: *Once the evidence and messages were given, I told Lisa who it was (Sprite). Lisa was shocked as she had met Rob at my event the Saturday before the Monday Sprite passed and she bought his books. She read about Buzz and that's the reference she was given. This could have been Buzz helping or her reference that this dog was connected to the author of the book. This will be something she'll learn to discern by practicing.*

*Lisa was shocked to know it was Rob and Tom's dog and after thinking about it for a minute, everything fell into place for her… she had scheduled this appointment 3 weeks prior to Sprite's passing, was at the event for a reason and bought the books from the owner of this mysterious barking pup, which could be used for references later.*

*It was a complete and unexpected "circle." It was a set up event by spirit… everything fell into place.* That's how spirits work. Even spirits of our beloved pets!

**A Message to me from Sprite**

After reading the messages and talking with Ruthie and Troy about Sprite, I was finally able to let go of the feelings of guilt over letting him go. Just a few days after Sprite's passing, we were returning home from running an errand when I received my first communication from Sprite.

We were in our pick-up truck with our three other dogs riding in the back seat. I began getting my usual headache which alerts me that a spirit (or ghost) is present. At that moment I heard, "squeety mouse." It's a silly made up nickname that I gave to Sprite because he would make a noise that I called "squeeting" when he was picked up or held. I sensed right away that Sprite's spirit was present with us, riding in the backseat with our other three dogs, as he once did. I began to tear up knowing that he remembered our time together and thought enough of us to return to let us know he was alright.

## Sprite's Butterflies

As I mentioned in a previous chapter, butterflies are one way that a spirit (animal or human) can let us know that they're around us. Sprite sent a yellow and black butterfly around to also show us that he's with us, or anyone that thinks about him.

Three days after Sprite passed, Tom and I took our three dogs (two Dachshunds and a Weimaraner) out for a walk. That's when we got a sign that Sprite was with us. Toward the end of the walk, a yellow and black butterfly flew near all three dogs. Although it was July, we had not seen a butterfly the entire season, so it was unusual to see one. There were two other aspects of this visit that were unusual. First, it's unusual for a butterfly to fly near dogs. Second, the dogs didn't go after it. They just watched it. It was as if they heard Sprite telling them "I'm here."

All of us just watched that beautiful butterfly and I took several pictures of it. The butterfly just stayed on the grass near the dogs and didn't move. I knew it was a message from Sprite that he is fine and regained 100% health as a spirit. We were all happy to see this wonderful sign from Sprite.

**(Sprite's Butterfly appeared to us many times. Credit: Rob G.)**

Spirits sometimes use butterflies or other insects to convey that they're around. Because my grief was blocking out Sprite's messages he found another way to get the messages to me. If you are still grieving, grief will block out their signs. Some spirits are strong and persistent, like Sprite, and will give visible signs they're okay.

Sometimes spirits will use butterflies, birds, feathers, flowers, pennies or other signs to convey that they're around us and thinking of us.

Our pets know who loves them and also knows to come to people whom they know will share messages. In one case, Sprite's spirit traveled over 1,000 miles to get the message to me.

**Sprite's Butterfly Visits Jill**

On July 22, I received an email from our friend Jill. She also got a visit from Sprite's spirit in the form of the same kind of butterfly that Sprite used to communicate with us. Jill wrote: *"Just had to tell you that I was sitting out back on a lounge chair on Saturday. Not five minutes after reading your blog on Sprite, a yellow and black butterfly rested on my abdomen. Unfortunately, I didn't realize what it was at first and I moved, sending it away. But, I have seen it multiple times between our yard our neighbors' yard over the weekend!*

*Nine days later Jill got another sign from Sprite. She said: I was at a meeting on the 5th floor of our office yesterday afternoon and a yellow and black butterfly came to the window and looked in.* She knew it was Sprite.

## Sprite's Butterfly Visits Layla

My friend Layla is a huge dog-lover who lives in the western U.S. She read the news about the passing of our dog Sprite and realized that she had also been visited by him.

Layla wrote: *When I was in Santa Fe, I saw this exact butterfly around the middle of July in front of my friend's Art Gallery on Canyon Road. The butterfly was very large and stayed with me for quite a while as I was working on the Day lilies in the garden. I don't usually attract butterflies, however, mostly every Hummingbird within miles finds me! Perhaps it was the spirit of your Sprite. Santa Fe is pure magic you know!*

From time to time, both my partner and I have sensed Sprite's presence in our house. We can tell where he's walking around, or if he's just laying down watching us and our other three dogs. Every night before I go to bed, I always say goodnight to Sprite and our late friend Ed, both of whose photos are hanging on our wall next to each other.

## Other Spirits Confirm Sprite is With Them

Earlier I mentioned that I asked three spirits to help Sprite as he crossed over in the vet's office: Our friend Ed, my dad, and my puppy Buzz. All three spirits acknowledged they were there at the time, and two of them acknowledged that Sprite was with them, by providing us with pennies with meaningful years on them.

One week after Sprite's passing, my partner and I were getting out of our car in a parking lot, and he found a penny. The penny was dated 1996, the year that Ed passed. That penny let us know that Ed was in fact there in the room when Sprite passed, and the Sprite is safe with him.

That same week that we found Ed's penny, I received a confirmation from my dad that Sprite was happy, healthy and with him and the others. I was getting out of my car at Dunkin' Donuts to get a morning coffee. Sitting on the ground right outside of the driver's side door was a shiny penny. Like Ed's penny had the year that he passed, this penny had the year my dad passed: 2008.

## Conclusion

What is remarkable about the messages received from the mediums is that while each of them received the same messages from Sprite about being "bouncy and energetic" on the other side, each of them also received a separate and unique message that could only have come from Sprite – identification of the dish, the blanket, and the red ball and rope toy. It was then that without feelings of sorrow or remorse, I could finally get messages from Sprite.

These mediums, who are also close friends of ours, have helped us resolve the feelings of guilt that we harbored for being an active participant in Sprite's passing. They helped us obtain peace of mind through confirmation of each other's messages.

If you are a pet owner and you have to make that intractable choice for your pet, I encourage you to seek out a learned medium to help you in your time of grief. Once the time of grieving has passed, it is then that we begin to realize that our pets are continually with us, even in Spirit, and their unconditional love will continue to live on.

## CHAPTER 7: MAN AT THE ANIMAL HOSPITAL

I decided to include this short story because so many of us have either already felt this way, or will have these feelings when the time comes to say goodbye to our companion pets.

The night before Sprite passed, he developed a nosebleed. Total fear and panic set in. For about an hour I tried every means I could think of to stop the bleeding, but to no avail.

By 10 p.m. I decided to take him to an emergency care veterinary clinic. The doctor came out and performed and initial examination before taking Sprite into an exam room.

As I was nervously sat in the waiting room, a man named James was also seated in the waiting room. He was inconsolable over having to make the decision to put down his 15 year old dog. The scene was heartbreaking. The doctor came out and escorted James into an exam room so that he could say his final goodbyes.

A short while later, James came back out into the waiting room, sobbing uncontrollably, and just standing by himself. I stood up, walked over to him, and gave him a hug. I told him that I was sorry for his loss, and he began to tell me his story.

It had been a sweltering hot day in July. James had been cleaning out the front seat of the car, and did not see his small dog crawl into the back seat. He had gone about his day, totally oblivious to the fact that his dog had been in the back seat of the car with the windows rolled up, the entire day. She eventually succumbed to heat exhaustion.

After I talked with him for a minute, I gave him my card, explained to him that I was a medium, and that sometimes dogs will communicate with the living after they have passed. Of course when I do such things, I always run the risk of something thinking that I am totally out of my mind. But I really wanted to help James.

Three days later, I received a short email from him:

*I am in so much pain over losing my little girl/ jpw.*

Another day passed, and I received a message from his beloved dog, so I responded back to James' initial email as follows:

*Hi James - Thanks for the email. I'm so sorry about your loss. The following evening, we had to say goodbye to our senior Dachshund, Sprite. He was 16 1/2 years old. The grief that I've endured over his loss blocked messages from him and others for the last couple of days.*

*However, your dog has given me some messages. It was her time to pass. She said that she was not feeling well, and crawled into the car knowing it was a safe place. She didn't want to make noise as she usually did because she didn't want to prolong her time here and cause you the pain of having to euthanize her.*

*She's showing me a rounded bed. Was that hers? She said she had a great life and you were the best parents. Although she knows that there will be regrets she doesn't want you to feel guilty. It was not your fault at all - she knew what she was doing. This was to avoid causing you pain, guilt and endless questioning to put her down later.*

*Please take her ashes and put them in a prominent place. She wants to let you know that if you talk to her, she can hear you. Sound is energy, and her spirit is now energy. She'll also try to give you signs that she's still around you.*

*You may hear her nails on the floor. The love you shared binds you together. I keep hearing "beef," and "bone." Either it's a beef bone, or they're two separate things that meant something special to her. Did you make beef for her? She appreciated the kind ways that you treated her. She said she did not start out that way. Did you rescue her or was she ill as a pup?*

*Please feel free to write me back. I'll do what I can to help you get through the grief. Please know that her strongest message is that you should NOT feel guilt. It was her time to go. She needed to spare you the pain of making a decision to euthanize her. I get that message very, very strongly. Sending a hug to you. Rob*

A week passed with no response from James. Then on July 17, I received the following email from him:

*Hello and thank you. I cooked her dinner every night. She has a round bed. I will place her ashes in her bed. I was a mess for 5 days. She was my little girl.*

I was so glad to be able to pass a message on to James.

# CHAPTER 8: Q&A ABOUT ASHES OF PETS

Many people choose to retain the ashes of their beloved pets, myself included. In our home, we have the ashes of both Buzz and Sprite, side by side, along with framed photographs of them in life next to each cremation wooden box.

Having a cremation box or urn with a pet's ashes can draw the spirit of a pet. A pet's energy may linger and continue to be attached to their ashes. Energized by our love for them, that emotional energy is capable of enabling their spirit to come through to us and give us signs and messages after their passing.

Ashes can be likened to a spiritual magnet. As long as that emotional energy remains heightened by love, it provides the ability for a spirit to manifest itself in sight, sound, or in other ways. But that doesn't mean that your pet's spirit will linger in your home. They'll only come when they have something to tell you, or to comfort you when you need comforting.

**(Sprite's & Buzz's ashes with pictures & toys. Credit: R.Gutro)**

Earlier in this book, I related the story of my friend Craig's boxer, Oprah, who provided that amazing message to him conveyed by a grouping flowers arranged in the shape of a heart. Oprah also provided an auditory sign in the very same room where her ashes are kept. Craig's friend, Jim, was in Craig's house waiting for him to return. Jim heard the distinctly recognizable sound of Oprah's toenails clicking on the hardwood floors. No one else was in the house at the time other than Jim.

I receive some interesting questions by email and through social media. In keeping with the subject matter of this chapter, I would like to share a couple of them specifically dealing with pet's ashes, reprinted here along with my responses.

**QUESTION:** If a pet's spirit leaves their body immediately when they die, then how can a pet owner keep the spirit of the pet close to them, especially if the pet dies at the vet's office and not at home? I would hate to think of my pet's spirit being lost at the vet's office and not able to find me. Do you have any thoughts on this?

**ANSWER:** Often when a pet passes, a human loved one is waiting to receive them on the other side, and to guide them as they cross over. Once on the other side, our pets know where we are. They know where their home is located. They know where to find us because of the love we have for them. That love acts as a beacon shining out to them, helping them to locate us. That's exactly how all of our late loved ones animal and human can find us after they pass.

At our Sprite's "final" vet appointment, I asked for two people that we know in Spirit, accompanied by my puppy, Buzz, to come and guide little Sprite as he crossed over. I felt the telltale sign from Spirit – a column of cold at each elbow – and I knew that my request has been granted. At the moment of Sprite's passing, I was absolutely sure that he was welcomed on the other side by family. Everyone should ask their loved ones to help their pets cross into the light when it is our pet's time to go.

Love is an energy, a beacon that empowers spirits, whether human or animal, to find us. Be especially vigilant around special dates such as birthdays, anniversaries, or a day that may have been special to your late pet, like the day of adoption or the day of passing.

**QUESTION 2:** Do I need to move ashes? What about dreams [I may have] of my pets?

My beloved cat Barney (my best friend of 16 years) passed and I have his ashes in my bedroom on my desk. Now I have been touched twice on my leg and back. Last night it woke me up, [it felt like] two fingers pressed down on my leg twice. The last time something rubbed my lower back twice with what seemed to be fingers as well.

Barney was a gentle sweet soul and I get the vibe that this is a woman's energy touching me. I paid extra money to have just his ashes in the box. It is a small sealed box.

It is so frightening and I'm also having nightmares about once a week. This could be from my chronic pain, I don't know. But the visitations actually wake me up and I don't want it to happen again. I don't understand why I am being touched; I don't feel it is evil but trying to connect with me.

Should I move his box out of my place into my storage? The thought makes me sad since I wanted him near me. He has visited me in dreams to comfort me and was young and healthy again. I know this is something else.

**ANSWER:** It is very likely that Barney has come back to let you know he is around. I think that it is because he knows that you are in pain, and wants to provide comfort and companionship as he did when he was alive. Cats will often come back and curl up on the bed with the parents, even after they have passed.

If you are uncomfortable, I would suggest bringing his ashes into another room and telling him that "mom is okay," and that you appreciate his concern, but you need to sleep. You can always tell him to visit you during the day. There is nothing to fear about his visitations. The fact that you do not sense anything evil or bad is a good sign, and one that indicates the spirit is one who is benign or in fact, cares about you and your welfare.

Pets in Spirit are often drawn to their ashes, attracted by the love that we have for them, which brings them to us when we need them the most. In fact, you should be happy that he continues to come around to check on you; although, I would ask him to come around only during the daytime.

When we pass, the physical energies that were in our bodies, mesh with our minds/souls and personalities to form an entity of energy. If the energy continues in its earthbound state, then it is a ghost. If the energy crosses over into the light, it becomes a spirit. They were all living, breathing people or animals before, and they are nothing to fear after passing.

Barney has crossed over, but is making temporary check-ins because of your health. Just tell him to let you sleep. Barney has come into your dreams because it is the easiest way for spirits to communicate with us from the other side. When our logical minds are asleep, they can connect through dreams. It is our logical thinking that causes us to ignore signs from spirits and explain them as "coincidences" or something in the physical world.

NOTE: Since the writer moved the ashes in another room and asked Barney to stop, the sensations ceased, and she has been sleeping through the night.

# CHAPTER 9: RESCUED BY A DOG'S GHOST

The following story was provided by a friend and fellow a dog rescue volunteer. She's one of the most big-hearted, dog-dedicated people I know, and this is an amazing story of how a ghost or spirit dog rescued her when she was a girl. This story has never appeared anywhere else. It proves that even in the afterlife, pets (whether ours or someone else's pets) can come back and protect people.

### *I Was Rescued by a Dog's Ghost*

*By Shelley Sehnert*

*I am by training and vocation a scientist, so I try to rationalize any experience I have that seems to be "supernatural" Nevertheless, and I know there are people who think it is all coincidence, I have had several strong, accurate premonitions. I do not discount them, but I don't know what to do with them either. For example, I knew my healthy, young, never sick a day in her life sister had cancer and what sort of cancer weeks before it was diagnosed. I knew. I even told my mother, who was stunned when the doctor told her the same thing.*

*This narrative is true, I lived it, and this is the first time I have written about it.*

*I grew up on Alsenborn Farm, an old plantation south of the Mason-Dixon Line way out in the country in Maryland. The farm was named for the long dead owner's favorite dog. The big white clapboard house stood at the end of an alley flanked by tulip poplars that had grey trunks and fragrant, thick-petaled blossoms in the spring. I used to climb up into the branches of these trees as a very young child since they forked low and the branches were wide and the trees silent and calm. Those trees had been brought in by train, one descendent of this wealthy family having been a railroad executive. They were perhaps never small.*

*The outbuildings that had been barns filled with sheep and cattle were decaying and the fences falling apart except for the yard where the heifers were kept. Graceful lanes curved between old sheds, barns, and the carriage house. We lived in the carriage house, above the area where the carriages had once been kept, right by a large barn that had housed the horses that pulled them down those now-paved lanes to the main road, a shady, shadowy ride filled with light filtering through the 100 year old trees. Fairies were said to live in the roots of some of those old lady trees and the leaves were broad, the ground covered with acorn caps for the elves to wear in the autumn.*

*From our front door you could see a yellow clapboard house with green shutters and a low front porch that might have been where the property manager once lived. Between the house and our front door was a long yard, a large hedge, and the wind tearing through, whipping the leaves into a swirl in the winter, wind that sat heavy and thick in the summer sun as the weeds grew quickly in the heat, trying to grow and make seeds.*

*I was 4 years old, and almost 5 that late autumn, and I was still an only child, the baby after me having been born too early and died and the brother after him not yet conceived.*

*I played alone wherever I wanted on the old 100 acre farm, wandering over a brook that led to a moss covered spring filled swimming pool, the diving board waiting to bounce with the leap of a diver, up hills, into pastures, anywhere I wanted to go. I loved it, I love it still. Even though long ago the bulldozers took it all away, the trees still sway in my memory, the green awnings flap-flap, the ice crystals fall now and then in the early winter late fall days of November.*

*I made my dolls wear coats and played outside in the curve of an old patio near the big house, now azalea and boxwood overgrown, the mortar cracked and missing between the flagstones. Mama was in the house doing chores. She would ring the bell when it was time for lunch and we would have soup and crackers in the kitchen while the potatoes boiled, surrounded by clean laundry, piled in baskets. An apple cut into thin slices would follow.*

*I don't know where they came from, those dogs, those silent, sleek, slim black dogs, so many, 6 maybe 7, their breath and mouths were all I could see and I was too surprised to be afraid, too quickly knocked over on the ground. My brown car coat had plastic buttons shaped like logs on the cuffs and down the front, and I could see one of the buttons on my sleeve pulled between a dog's teeth as he ran over me, onto me, I could smell his warmth, the smell of warm animal, and heard the growling, long and low and deep matching my own sudden crying, soft and sudden, the breath of the dogs all over me filling my face.*

*And then I heard the barking, the different sound of barking, loud, close, not one of these Dobermans, but different, very close, defensive, urgent, so urgent, demanding and as quickly the Dobermans were off me and running and turning and going back and then fast away from the barking of the big black German shepherd who stood by me, six feet or so away, barking, barking, barking as if saying: "Away, Get Away, Get Away, Mine, Mine, Mine, My Child, My Child, Get Away, Away, Away!!!!"*

*We didn't have a dog.*

*I got my first dog for my fifth birthday that same winter, the best birthday present I had ever been given, ever would be given, a miniature poodle puppy. Seventeen years later she took my heart with her to heaven.*

*We lived on the farm until I was 10, and my childhood was snatched away when we moved closer to the city. The apple press stored in an old barn was too heavy to take and was likely demolished when the barn and carriage house were knocked down to make the land lie flat, the lanes gone, the old oak ladies now firewood and flooring and fences. I couldn't bear to think about the tulip trees and stayed in them as long as I could. The owner, the last of her long line, had sold it to pay for her old age, the heifers auctioned. Even in her 70s she would walk every morning at 6 a.m. in a black bathing suit and fur trimmed boots to feed them and then walk to that spring fed swimming pool in the glade to swim.*

*In the worst of winter she would take an axe with her and chop a hole in the ice so she could swim. She never wore a hat but she did wear a short barn coat. But now she was in her 80s and all that was left of her and the heifers was their warm scent, the remembered sound of their happy, hungry breakfast.*

*I said goodbye to all my favorite places, the fields where digging produced special rocks, the pastures filled with sweet clover that made lovely beds for watching clouds, the fairies in the tree roots, the brook, chattering in the early spring about robins and sunshine.*

*And then there was the flagstone patio, where six years earlier I had nearly been mauled to death by a pack of Doberman Pinchers. Near the patio, at the end of the tulip tree alley, behind the azaleas and over grown boxwoods, flush with the ground, was a small, smooth gravestone. I brushed away the leaves and it read: ALSIE. [I believe that was the name of the dog's ghost that protected me].*

## CHAPTER 10: MEDIUM RUTHIE LARKIN'S DOG BOSTON

---

Several friends are developed and learned mediums and they have received messages from pets. They've graciously allowed me to share some of their stories. The mediums include Ruthie Larkin, the "Beantown Medium," Barb Mallon, my mentor, and Troy Cline, my fellow medium in the Inspired Ghost Tracking group.

This chapter was written by medium Ruthie Larkin about her messages from Boston, her own late, beloved dog and great canine communicator.

Ruthie received many messages from her late dog that came in many ways. By reading the messages that she received, you may be able to recognize the messages you get from your own beloved pet.

Ruthie Larkin's dog named Boston was a Shih Tzu and was her daughter in every respect for 14 ½ years. Boston was born on Sept. 9, 1997 and passed on June 5, 2012. Here's what Ruthie said about her dog:

*I always referred to her as the daughter that never gave me a moment's problem. She and I were connected immediately. I can remember taking her for puppy training lessons when she was about 4 months old and she would not let the dog trainer take her and would not leave my side. In fact, she was already sticking to me like glue. She loved many other people but there was no one like her Mommy.*

**(Ruthie Larkin holds her beloved Boston. Credit: R.L).**

*Boston had an instinct for what I was going to do before I even made a move. If we were resting on the sofa, it was as if she was reading my mind and she would get up and get ready to move while I was still thinking of it. She would already start to move from one room to another before I started walking toward the place that she somehow magically knew I was heading to.*

*She also knew when she would be going with me in the car and when she would not and this is way before I made a move to get her leash. She would settle herself down in the hall by the garage looking at me with her big brown sad eyes when she knew she was not going to go in the car. She would do this long before the time she should have realized that she was not going. It was as if this little 16 pound dynamo read my mind!*

*She completed my life in so many ways. I never felt alone no matter what had happened in my life or what went wrong. I always knew my little girl would be waiting for me with her winning ways and loving eyes. She would get so excited to see me when I returned from being at work or on errands. It was always a joy to come home to this little bundle of love. I will forever miss her and I make sure I kiss her little collar each day and look at her picture and tell her that I love her. By the way, somehow her collar still magically has her scent on it!*

### Boston Comes Through to Ruthie Many Times

*Boston passed on June 5, 2012 at 11:10 a.m. EDT.*

*The first sign from Boston in the afterlife was her inspiration to my sister to send me an email at the time Boston passed. The email, which I read later that night, was dated June 5 at 11:23 a.m. EDT from my sister Patty. The email was all about going into God's light when we pass. As I read it, I realized that she had sent it to me right around the actual time of Boston's passing. I know that it was orchestrated by Boston.*

*On June 5, 2012 at 2:10 p.m. EDT, I had been crying almost constantly since Boston left the house with our vet. I was talking on the phone with my friend Donna and listening quietly to her experience of getting a sign from her dog Brandy after she had passed. Right in the middle of her story, I heard the spirit of my late sister Mary Ellen shout very loudly "I've got her!" She then showed me a vision of her playing with Boston. I was so relieved because I'm sure Mary Ellen's spirit had been trying to get through to me since Boston had passed, so she had to shout!*

*Just five minutes later at 2:15 p.m. EDT, when I was still talking with Donna, I walked into my bedroom and immediately saw the baby monitor had been completely turned around in the cradle. I walk by that monitor often and always notice it. It was not turned around before. I am very particular about my home and the items displayed in it and would have seen that it was not properly sitting in the cradle. I believe this was also a sign from Boston and Mary.*

*The next day, June 6 at 8:20 a.m. EDT, - I was pulling out of my garage with my grandson Levi to go to his school. I looked back at the house and I did a double take, as a pair of dark eyes were looking out of Boston's window by the door, just like she used to do when I left and returned home! Although I later realized it was Levi's toy car which has eyes, I definitely think that was another sign from Boston. She likely influenced him to leave the car there to simulate her watching out the window. I know there is no such thing as coincidence.*

*That same night at 9:30 p.m. EDT, I was sitting on the floor eating dinner and watching TV and all of a sudden I felt Boston's energy right beside me. I placed my hand down to see if I could feel her energy and I definitely felt it. She used to sit there every time I ate my dinner on the coffee table which was most every night. She always patiently waited for handouts which I always gave her. The feeling was strong and it lasted for about 5 minutes. I even put my hand down and patted her.*

*The next visit came three days later on Saturday, June 9 at 11:30 a.m. EDT. I had been reading in my bed and was thinking and missing Boston a lot. I finally got up to go to my laptop and research ADC's (after death communications) from pets. While I was sitting in my office I heard her do her one bark. She would always do that when I disappeared from the bed. I also heard her do a bark when I was upstairs writing this, and the bark came from downstairs! I can't remember the exact date and time but it was before this time.*

*On June 10 at 5:20 a.m. EDT, I was just beginning to wake when I heard very clearly one loud Boston bark. It jolted me awake just like it used to. There were times she used to do that when she was in bed with me and she needed water or had to go potty or just wanted me awake with her. I quickly opened my eyes and said "thank you Boston."*

*That same night around 6:37 p.m. EDT, I was laying on the couch, watching television and drifting off for a cat nap when I distinctly once again heard one very loud Boston bark. She would do that all the time when I was just about to fall asleep on the couch as she would either want me to take her out or she would want to get up on the sofa. She is definitely paying me visits.*

*On June 11, 2012 at 8:52 a.m. EDT, I was reading in bed and heard Boston's tags jingle on her collar as if she was actually in bed with me. That used to happen often if she was losing patience and wanted to go downstairs. It was her message that she was ready to leave our bed. Her collar was sitting right next to me and had not moved so this noise came from beyond. I also got the feeling that she was trying to communicate with me and then I realized the spirit of my sister Mary Ellen was also trying to come in. I could not make it happen though. I have problems with spirits trying to communicate with me when they're from my own life.*

*Boston's next message came on June 17 at around 8 p.m. EDT. It was Father's Day. Earlier in the day I had brunch with Dick, Denny, Reilly, Donna, Vernon and Brian. Our new Soul Sister Ibelle also dropped in. Denny, Reilly and Ibelle had all gone home and the rest of us were sitting around the dining room table having dessert and coffee. Vernon was talking to me and all of a sudden I felt Boston's energy between Dick and me. I'm sure she came to pay Dick a visit on his special day. I gave him a homemade card from Boston with her picture on the front as well as a box of homemade chocolate chip cookies from her.*

*On June 29 at 10:50 a.m. I dropped Boston's original urn with her ashes off at Medway Animal Hospital. I had purchased her new beautiful urn and they were going to have the transfer made. I donated the original urn to a needy family who has lost a pet.*

*Anyway, I was in an exam room with Melissa going over the directions with her and upon opening the door to leave and go into the hall there was a family with a Shih Tzu puppy who was only 11 weeks old. My heart melted and of course I had to hold him. He proceeded to cover my entire face with puppy kisses. I told the family (Mom with 2 kids) what a wonderful companion the little guy would make. I walked out with tears in my eyes as I knew this was another sign from Boston sending me her love. All the many, many times I've been there I have never seen a Shih Tzu puppy!*

*On July 1 at 7:59 a.m. I was in my bathroom putting on make-up preparing for a day of scrapping with Jeannine and I heard Boston bark her one bark. That's exactly what would have happened because I had been gone from the bed long enough and she wanted to be with me. I thought "Thank you, Boston for another wonderful sign. I love getting signs even if they are spread out a little more now."*

*Two days later on July 3 it was 12:09 a.m. when I was folding clothes in the laundry room when again, I heard Boston's one bark. It sounded as if it was coming from downstairs.*

*Several weeks passed before I received another sign from Boston. On July 21 at 2:17 a.m. I was doing some catching up on my laptop and decided to update my log for my grandson Levi. I update it at least once a week. I went into his log to update and found the following text already there:*

> 6/5 – 6/6/2012 (Tuesday 11:30 AM – Wednesday 9:30 AM) – Today I had to help Boston transition to Rainbow Bridge. Two of our local vets came to the house around 10:30 AM so I did not pick up Levi until 4:30 PM. Dick came over and we sent out for dinner. Levi did cheer us up but our spirits were most certainly heavy with sadness.

*This is most definitely another sign from my little girl as there is no reason in the world that it should appear in Levi's July log. This text is from Levi's log list from June, which is in another document altogether. Unbelievable! Thank you Boston and thanks to Mary Ellen for continuing to help her send me signs. I miss you so much and am always thinking of my little girl.*

*On July 25 around 3:15 p.m. EDT, I was sitting in a chair at my hairdressers while my hair was taking on color. I was reading a magazine and was very tired and momentarily fell asleep. I clearly saw Boston sitting in my lap and she was facing outward just like she always liked to be held. She was in unbelievably beautiful condition, as her white was as white as snow and she gave the impression of supreme health. I have not dreamed of Boston since she passed and this was like a very clear vision between true sleep and wakefulness. Another sign for sure. Thank you Boston once again for showing me how you are doing. This time I felt more peace afterwards and upon returning home also felt better about everything. I usually feel overwhelming sadness when I return home and she isn't there to greet me. Upon walking into the house I immediately thought of that vision and was comforted.*

*A week later on Aug. 1, 2012, I dreamed that Boston had appeared to me and I was really able to kiss and hug her and give her a lot of affection. She was also able to communicate with me in telepathic language and we were having a conversation. She was happy and youthful and running around like a puppy. I went to wake my sister Donna up to tell her because I wanted her to see what I was seeing and just as I was doing that Boston disappeared from my arms. When Donna woke up I was telling her and Boston started to appear again so Donna was also able to see her. It was such a beautiful dream. Once again, I felt a strong sense of peace afterwards and know this was also an ADC and not just a dream.*

*Months passed before the next sign from Boston came on Dec. 22, 2012. I had a dream that I saw Boston in the yard. It was not the place where I live today but a place that I have dreamed about before. It was a home on the water and it had a beautiful wall where large lions and tigers walked along the wall. In my dream I had been locked out of my house and I was going to get my extra set of keys from my neighbor's house (John and Marie) and I thought I saw a small cat run into my yard. I went to check on it, as I feared that one of the large cats would get it. Upon going around to the side of my yard, I saw Boston as clear as day. Boston was so happy and as I kept getting closer, she started to fade into a beautiful small white light that came to me. I knew for a fact it was her energy and was so happy that once again I was able to see her.*

*On January 6, 2013, Michelle and Dick had just picked up my grandson Levi to take him to the doctors, as I was not feeling great and needed to rest. I had been watching Levi for several days in a row because Michelle had an appendectomy and couldn't take care of him. However, I had not yet recuperated from walking pneumonia. I was lying on the sofa and had fallen asleep. I was awakened with Boston doing her little whining, which she used to do all the time the moment I fell asleep on the couch, as she wanted to be picked up to be put on the other sofa.*

*On April 21, 2013, Boston came back with a physical sensation. I was in the bathroom getting ready for a Reading with a family who had lost a son and I was as usual rushing around. I started to go into my bedroom to get dressed and then turned around quickly to go back into the bathroom as I had forgotten something. When I did that, I felt Boston was at my feet and I almost tripped over her which would have been nothing new as she always followed me so closely. Her energy was overwhelmingly strong and it seemed so real that I immediately sat down on the boudoir chair and had tears in my eyes. I still miss her so very much and it is still so hard not to have her with me.*

*In the summertime, on Aug. 11, 2013, I was staying at my friend Donna's place for the weekend when I very clearly saw a flash of white light close to the floor before I went to bed. I knew in my heart that it was Boston. I always took her with me to Donna's and she was always close by in my room.*

Obviously Boston's spirit is around Ruthie and the love draws them together. Now that you've read Ruthie's experiences with Boston, you can now recognize those kinds of messages from your late pets. There is no such thing as a coincidence. Spirits make things happen for a reason - which is usually to help the living.

# CHAPTER 11: MEDIUM BARB MALLON'S DOG BLUE

This chapter was written by medium Barb Mallon about her messages from Blue, her own late, beloved dog and great canine communicator. Barb wrote this soon after her family said goodbye to Blue, and later added to it as Blue made more appearances.

*Many people believe animals do not have souls, and therefore cannot connect or communicate after their passing as people will. This is simply not true. There are thousands upon thousands of accounts of after death communications (ADC's) with passed pets, and as a medium, it's not uncommon for me to connect to a clients' animal in spirit, as well. I know it's so comforting to hear, and I was truly hoping the same thing would happen for me and my family with the passing of our sweet 15 year old Australian Shepherd named Blue.*

*The thing is, while I link with OTHER peoples' "spirit people and animals," I rarely have an ADC from my own loved ones in spirit! I HAVE had two very vivid dreams of my grandfather, after he passed, and they were indeed communications. I could feel the electrical energy and hear him speaking, and the dreams have stuck with me as if I had them yesterday.*

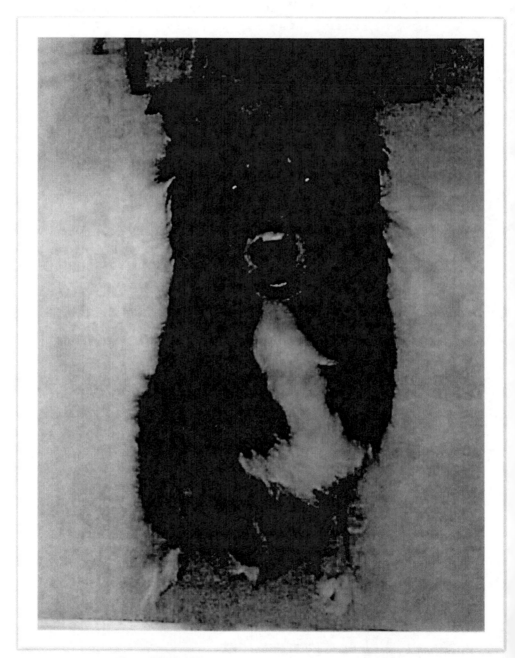

(Barb Mallon's dog, Blue. Credit: B. Mallon)

128

*When we had to put our wonderful Labrador, Sammy to sleep 15 years ago, I hoped for ADC's from him, but never really had any. I did see him unexpectedly in a meditation, so I know that was a little hello, but I really wanted more. I guess he just needed to go and do his thing. :) My kids have seen him, but I've never had that clear connection feeling, personally.*

*When we had to put Blue down, I wasn't very confident she would visit. She was so depressed before she left (except for the sudden turn-around in the vets office, which made it even harder to put her to sleep!), had awful arthritis in her back hips, slept all day, was just skin and bones and just couldn't be a dog anymore. This is why we felt she needed leave this physical plane; it was just too hard to see her like that another day.*

*I felt horrible making that decision, just as anyone does, and went home and cried all night about it. I didn't sleep well and felt emotionally and physically spent the next day. My kids stayed home from school, and my husband was emotionally drained. It was not a good day.*

*In the evening, we sat as a family watching TV and just trying to focus on some kind of normalcy for a while. My son, Bren was quietly trying to solve his new Rubik's cube when something*

**129**

*banged right into our Christmas tree, and it shook hard. A large ornament fell to the ground, and we all sat there watching in disbelief ornaments swinging wildly back and forth. There was no physical reason this would happen. No one was near the tree and nothing could have caused that commotion. We knew it was Blue, because she would constantly walk over to the tree with her e-collar on, bang into it and knock down ornaments. She did this the last day she was here before we left for the vet's office.*

*That, alone brought me some peace, but not nearly as much as what happened in the early hours on one morning that followed.*

*It snowed here a bit in Virginia, and I received a text from the school at 5 a.m. saying there was a two hour delay. I re-set my alarm for 9 a.m., curled up and went back to sleep. I then drifted into such a vivid dream. I was in my kitchen and my husband and kids were swirling around me (think we were making dinner or something). Suddenly, Blue was at my feet, and my first reaction was to say, "Blue, watch out... go lay down" like I'd say when she stood smack in the middle of things. Then, it hit me, Blue had passed away, yet here she is! I said, "BLUE!!! Hi Blue!!! Look at you!" She was so excited and had her full tail (it apparently had been lopped off and was just a nub in life) and it was wagging crazily.*

*She was always called the smiling dog, and she was looking up at me smiling and so excited. I reached down to grab her and realized I could feel her! She was physical. Her fur was beautiful and shiny, smooth and brushed. She was at her "chubby" weight again, all filled out, soft, excited and happy. She looked and acted exactly the same as after she had a bath, was brushed and clean, and felt SO good about herself! I said, "Mike, boys, can you see her? Blue is RIGHT HERE!! LOOK!!" And they all knew and saw that I could see her, but they weren't able to. It was frustrating, but I hugged her, rubbed her belly and just soaked in how wonderful she felt. It was amazing.*

*There was a second scene, as if she tried again. Again, in the kitchen, I was doing the dishes and my husband Mike was to my right. I turned around to grab a pot off the stove, turned back and Blue was half in the sink and half on the counter. My initial reaction was, "Blue, what are you doing in the sink!?! Get down." Then I realized she had passed and I was so excited to see her. I wanted to get her off the counter and thought she'd be heavy because of her size, but when I went to pick her up, she was weightless. I brought her to the floor and rubbed and hugged her. Again, I screamed, "do you all see her? Blue is right here!!"*

*No one else saw her, but this time, my husband sat on the floor with me and I brought Blue over to him. He couldn't see her but rubbed her where I told him to, and Blue loved it. I could see he was scratching around her ears and rubbing her tummy, but he couldn't; even so, he was so happy and emotional and so was Blue. Then, she stood up and walked into the dining room.*

*Suddenly, another Blue was standing right next to her. I believe this was her brother, who I could have adopted with Blue, but we just didn't have the room... they were identical. They walked towards the Christmas tree and disappeared. When I looked at the carpet, they had left paw prints and Mike and the boys COULD see those and knew then she had really been there.*

*I woke up and just was amazed at how I felt. I knew she was back in her healthy body and was okay. I then felt that I wasn't alone in the room and there was someone near me.*

*Blue used to do this thing with everyone when she was healthy. She'd sit right next to you and if you weren't giving her attention, she'd take one paw and whap you on the arm or knee. Like a "hey, I'm here, pet me!" I felt her paw whap me just like that on my leg and then when I didn't move she did it again. It was lighter, of course, but I felt it. Then I felt her lay near the bed like she always did. She'd plop down, hit the bed and make it shake. It always scared me, then. This morning it was so comforting.*

*I know that was her way of saying goodbye and letting us know that all was well and she was OKAY... not just OKAY, but BETTER! After such a hard decision and after seeing her so miserable, it truly brought me peace. Thank you, my Blue doggie... we love and miss you so much.*

*In June of 2013, we had other little "Blue visits." A few times, I've seen movement in the spot she always laid, and I distinctly heard her unusual bark ("awf" rather than a normal bark). My younger son saw her briefly out in the snow and my other son dreamed of her and saw her happy and healthy as I did. :)*

*Throughout the years, my son Brady has seen Blue's spirit laying around various places in our home many times. This just happened the other day when he was walking home from school. He saw a black dog in the window looking at him and thought it was one of our pups, but dogs were in their crates at the time. :) He came in the door and saw the dogs and realized it couldn't be them... it was Blue! :)*

One of the easiest ways for spirits to communicate with us is through our dreams. That's because when we sleep our logical minds (that would try and explain happenings instead of understanding the message) are also "asleep" opening us up to messages.

## CHAPTER 12: MEDIUM TROY CLINE SHARES "PETE'S STORY"

This chapter was written by medium Troy Cline, who works with me in the Inspired Ghost Tracking group. Troy shared this story of how he connected to his boyhood dog Pete after 30 years, and how Pete's spirit provided Troy with an amazing message to relieve him of guilt he carried for all of that time.

*From the time that I was a little boy I had a great love and connection to dogs. I remember how much I loved going to my grandmother's farm in Jackson, Ohio, where I would be surrounded by a huge family of Beagles! I can still remember all of their names and personalities: Ginny the petite beagle mother of the beagle clan, Barney the awkward 'white' beagle with a brown patch over one eye, Jock the muscular beagle bother and Bruce the grumpy husky beagle grandpa. Oh yeah, and who could ever forget Tito; the only Collie of the family who would guard anything until he was verbally released him from his assignment. Toss in about 20 chickens, 5 geese, 4 hogs, 10 cows, 4 cats and any old barn with the best hay loft ever and BINGO....you had Grandma Baker's farm!*

*After a few years it became pretty clear that I had a growing fondness for beagles. Perhaps it was the countless beagle books that I bought at every school book fair that gave it away or my bedroom wall that was wallpapered with beagle posters of every kind? You can imagine the excitement I felt when my dad came home from work and announced that Ginny had given birth to her third litter of pups! I could tell from my dad's expression that one of the pups would be mine! 8 weeks later we made the 2 hour trip to Grandma Baker's farm where I was allowed to pick the beagle that would become my best friend for the next 12 years. Of course, I picked the runt of the litter: a beautiful grunting little blanket back beagle with one unique white stripe running down the back of his neck and brown ears that touched the ground. As it turned out my grandfather had already given him a name the seemed to stick ...Pete!*

*The next several years of my childhood would be spent teaching Pete how to hunt rabbits, shake hands, and play dead. He would in turn teach me how to howl at the sky, scratch his huge ears in just the right spots and run like crazy through the woods while he quickly sniffed everything in sight!*

*My dad's job as a minister meant that our family would have to move every 3-4 years. I must admit that it was rather exciting to move to different locations from time to time but it also meant that we would lose contact with most of our childhood friends and that at times could hurt deeply. I eventually grew a rather tough skin when it came to uncontrollable loss of friends and became rather good at shutting down the part of me that caused the pain. I must admit that having an amazing spiritually grounded mom, dad and little sister made those transitions much easier to take. However, it was my best friend Pete who kept me together when I felt alone or upset. I swear that dog could understand every word out of my mouth as I would sit on the ground next to his dog house, scratch his ears and talk through my problems.*

*As the years when by Pete little nose and ears became whiter with age but he never lost his gift of unconditional love. Finally the day came when I graduated from high school and moved on to Tennessee to attend my first college. I actually believe that my first year in college was the hardest year of my life and it's a miracle that I survived and am who I am today.*

*There were so many powerful changes happening in my life during that year. Most of my emotional energy was simply exhausted and I could no longer go into my back yard and explain everything to Pete while he would offer the gift of unconditional love. It was during that first year away from home that the protective mechanism I had acquired as a child 'kicked in' and enabled me to separate myself from those that I missed. Sadly to say, that included Pete. I knew my dad was taking care of him at home and that I would see him during my short visits but still, I became separated. (You can't imagine the giant lump in my throat right now as I write those words!)*

*Towards the end of my first year in college, I came home for a short visit. Pete had gotten loose from our back yard and was gone for most of the day. Since that had happened several times over the years and because we lived in the country, I wasn't too worried. I expected Pete to come home later that night completely exhausted from a day of unbridled running, chasing rabbits and sniffing! He never came home. At around 11 p.m. that night, my dad came home and called me to the bottom of the stairs. He then broke the news that Pete had been hit by a car and had been found dead along the side of a road about one-half mile from our house.*

*Oddly enough, I didn't feel anything. My emotions were...blank. I remember looking for my shoes and coat so that I could help my dad bury Pete along the river side where we played together. However, all of the emotional energy that I had repressed during that year came flooding back. My dad, understanding my grief, laid Pete's broken little body to rest for me.*

*For years I looked back at that moment with the deepest sense of guilt for allowing myself to become emotionally detached by my best friend. How could I ever forgive myself for not being there for him allowing myself to detach? Those answers would come in the most unexpected way years later while sharing my story with my good friend, Rob Gutro.*

*It was during lunch one day at work that Rob 'came out of the paranormal closet' and told me that he was a medium. Although I had come from a very evangelical family, I was very intrigued.*

*Over the years I had learned that all of us have unique gifts that come with a great variety of labels. In the Biblical world I'm known as a Seer with the gift of discernment. In the paranormal world, I'm known as a medium. We soon began to share what seemed to be an endless stream of paranormal experiences.*

*At one point in the conversation, Rob mentioned that he had the ability to connect with animals that had passed. I shared the story of my dog, Pete, and how I had carried a sense of guilt surrounding the year of his passing. Rob believed that if I opened myself up, I would be able to connect with Pete on my own. It had been over 30 years since Pete's passing and I had never connected with an 'animal' spirit in that way before so my expectations were rather low. However, the unexpected happened!*

*During my drive home from work I often spend time praying, singing and listening to podcasts. Some of my most powerful spiritual experiences have actually been behind the wheel of my car! If you see some crazy guy driving down the road, singing with tears running down his face, it's likely me! On my way home from work on the same day as my earlier lunch with Rob, I opened myself up in prayer and asked God about Pete and how he was doing. To my surprise the answer came in the most unexpected way. I sensed the presence of my little friend enter the car!*

*Pete was actually beyond excited to see me. I could actually sense his little 'white tipped' tail wagging furiously in the air with that all too familiar look of openness on his face. I was overwhelmed. The most amazing part of the experience was that HE WASN'T ANGRY! As a matter of fact he had NEVER been angry with me. It was at that moment that I learned what unconditional love meant! It was at that moment that I knew that there was nothing that I could have done that would have caused Pete stop loving me. It was at that moment that I shed all of over 30 years of guilt.*

*Pete paid me a few more unexpected visits after that with the same amount of excitement as his earlier visits. It was important to him that I believed the message he was allowed to share with me; the message of unconditional love. By the way, he also wanted me know that it's pretty awesome on the other side. Even for Beagles!*

# CHAPTER 13:   CATS AND OTHER COMMUNICATORS

---

Cats are another species of animal that I have received messages from in Spirit. Whether or not a species is capable of developing the ability to communicate with us from Spirit, I attribute to their ability to comprehend human language while here in the living world. In this chapter I will address experiences with cats first, and then to a lesser degree horses and birds. If I were to score capability of being able to communicate in the afterlife, it has been my experience that cats score very well, and rank right after dogs in their ability to develop the capability of communicating with us in Spirit.

## Cats:  Intelligence and Behavior

My friend Anne Marie said that her cats have learned and developed the habits and intelligence of a dog. She provided the following story about the intelligence of her cat Charlie (a.k.a. Charles Chaplin MacGuillicuddy).

Anne Marie writes:  *Charlie was born around April 1st, 1998 as far as I know.*

**(Charlie in clean laundry. Credit: AMC)**

*Charlie is "my first born," or less freakish sounding, he's my first pet I ever had on my own with four legs. (I'd previously had birds – parakeets, cockatiels and love birds – and I even had a rabbit once… in a 1 bedroom apartment. NOT a good idea!)*

*Charlie's my boy. Charlie is a rescue cat and was found by a dumpster at the Queen Mary in Long Beach, Calif. dying, left by his mother. He was rescued and I adopted him, sight unseen when*

*I heard about him. When I went to the vet's to pick him up (the vet had been nursing him back to health), she put him down on the counter, he walked straight over to me, and he offered me his paw.* [Editor's note: How many cats do you know offer their paw?] *Without using actual words, I believe he was saying, "Hi. I'm your new cat."*

*I realized that he looked like the famous Charlie Chaplin, and the name set in. (The MacGuillicuddy is a nod to Lucille Ball's character of Lucy, whose maiden name was MacGuillicuddy.) From the beginning, I treated Charlie like he was a dog, not a cat. And for the last 15 years, he's often behaved as a dog. He runs TO the door when someone knocks or comes in. He drinks out of the toilet. And when he was a kitten, he'd LOVE to drive around in the car with me.*

Your cat's behaviors in this world will be the same as a spirit to let you know he's still around, so pay attention!

**Cats Have Individual Personalities**

Anne Marie shared a story about another cat she has, who exhibits his own personality. As with humans, pets retain their personalities after they pass.  When her cat, "Spats," passes and comes back in spirit, he will be easily recognizable.

Anne Marie wrote:  *My other cat, Spats (a.k.a. Lord Spatsington) was born around April 1, 2004.*

*Spats was adopted from a rescue organization through Petco and given as a surprise to my husband Simon on our 6 month wedding anniversary. "Surprise, honey! It's a cat!"*

*I thought that Simon needed a cat because we could have a dog in our apartment and he's been a dog person. Spats came along and bonded with Simon.*

*In fact, the bond is very close. The two of them now regularly watch English Premier League Football on Saturday mornings, holding paws/hands, and Spats has totally become Daddy's Boy!*

*Spats can be a little sh\*t, but he's sweet as heck. He will take a swipe at our other cat Maddie and when we tell him off for doing so, he'll ever-so-innocently start a high-pitched and pathetic meow as if to say, "It wasn't me."*

*He loves to cuddle between our pillows at night and will take up half of Simon's pillow. (After all, Spats' theory is, what's yours is mine, and what's mine is mine.) He's greedy, and cheeky, and I love him to death. He always seems to be plotting his next maneuver. He has a very "entitled" personality, hence the name Lord Spatsington – he must believe he's royalty.*

*The bond he has with Simon is far stronger than the one with me, but if Simon's not around, I'll do for a pet, a scratch, whatever he deigns I can do for him. The minute I leave our sofa and Simon's on it, Spats will hop up to hang with Simon. He's hilarious!*

*With my cat Charlie, I realized how unique a personality a cat could have. Adding Maddie and Spats, it just amazed me how much of a personality they each have on their own. I never thought a cat could have a personality – thought that was really just a dog thing. I see now that it is an all-animal thing.*

Spats has a very strong personality; one that could easily be recognized as a spirit.

## A Catty Communication

I received an email communication from Doug who heard me speak at an event, and was grieving the loss of his cat. The following is an email exchange conveying the messages that I received from his cat, and Doug's responses.

Doug writes: *Last week, my girlfriend Sue and I had the sad responsibility of setting our 16-year-old-cat "Millie" free, after a diagnosis of hyperthyroidism and early-onset renal failure.*

*Even at the end, Millie seemed so full of life and enthusiasm, even with her body itself dying around her. Is there any way I could let her know I'm sorry for not being a better cat-"parent?" Sue and I are very hardworking, but sometimes it seemed that there was little we could give her (and our other cats) beyond all the love we could give her.*

*I just feel that I could (and should) have done better; I just don't know how. I just hope that she made it okay and that she's happy now. I hope she knows how much we miss her. Anyway, thank you very much for the books, and please feel free to write back.*

148

*PS:   I've been re-reading the "animal-spirits" sections of both your books.   They give me a great deal of comfort, but Millie's loss still hurts.*

*My Response:   Hi Doug- thanks for your note. My deepest sympathies to you and Sue Ellen on the passing of Millie.* [It was then that Millie started coming through to me while I was on the computer. That happens often, by the way].

*Millie does know how much you loved her. Do you have two other cats??* [I later found out that Millie only acknowledged the two cats she liked.] *They have watched her spirit come back and walk around. Keep an eye on them, and when it appears they're staring at nothing, they're seeing Millie.*

*What's with a rounded rug? I also get the sense that Millie liked the warmth from the dryer, when folding clothes.*

*Millie wants to convey that you DID take good care of her. She loved her life and you made the ultimate sacrifice of love to unselfishly not let her suffer any more. You are great cat parents.*

*Let me know if some of the things I got from her make sense. I get messages from pets and sometimes they're a challenge to decipher.*

Doug's Response: *You mentioned sensing two other cats in association with Millie. Had they passed on, or were they still alive? Sue Ellen and I actually have three other cats, and I find it unusual that Millie would have just mentioned two . . . Unless she were omitting "Bobby," our newest cat. Millie and Bobby didn't really "hit it off" during their brief time together. No fights, just lots of hissing.*

*Anyway, I've noticed at times all three cats stopping bolt-still in the middle of the room, staring at a point about three to five feet from them. I would see nothing, but I could sense their focus was completely centered there. I've also noticed one or more of our other cats focusing on our bedroom door (which we always leave open), yet still seeing nothing.*

*If the cats had passed on, the two might be Scotchie (Sue Ellen's first cat) and maybe Tigger, a neighbor's cat who had adopted our back porch as his center of operations, and whom we had gotten very fond of* [the cats were the two living cats they have, plus "Bobby" that Millie refused to acknowledge].

*The "rounded rug" was a bit of a poser, until I realized it may refer to a cat-tower Sue Ellen and I have in our bedroom. It stands about five feet tall with a large wooden drum near the base, two round shelves higher up and a circular "penthouse" at the very top. It's completely covered in deep-plush carpeting material. Millie spent a lot of her time lounging in that crow's nest, and we regarded it as sort of a "throne," although Chelly and Trekkie would use it on occasion when Millie wasn't around. Bobby is a Maine Coon cat, and is MUCH too big to get up there.*

My Response: *Thanks for the email. The two cats I mentioned are the ones that Millie got along with. Even on the other side, she still has "issues" with Bobby's behavior, but she'll work to correct them (as she sees them). That's why your cats stare at the open door. Millie makes appearances from time to time to "straighten out" Bobby's behavior!*

*The circular cat penthouse makes perfect or "purrfect" sense coming from Millie! That's why I got the message.*

What is interesting about this email exchange is that Millie conveyed her disapproval for Doug and Sue Ellen's third cat,

"Bobby," by not acknowledging him. Further, it took some detective work on Millie's parents' part to realize it was the rounded cat tower penthouse that she favored. Mediumship is like that. Mediums give message of things that were important to a spirit when they were alive, and the living have the task of determining what it is the spirit refers to.

## Melanie the Cat Remains Bonded to Her Mom

The following story was submitted by Terri about her precious cat Melanie:

Terri writes: *Melanie was my first real cat companion. She entered my life in 1974, when I was pregnant with my son. My roommate found the kitten behind a dumpster, skin and bones, all ears and nose. She brought it home for herself, but Melanie bonded with me. She spent much of the time sitting on my pregnant belly gazing into my eyes. We were soul mates. She birthed her first kittens while I nursed my son.*

*Melanie traveled with me from Wisconsin to New Jersey, via Amtrak, when I separated from my husband. When I drove back to Wisconsin for the divorce proceedings in a snow storm, she was in the van with me, including when we hit a slick spot and spun around on the highway, ending the right way at an exit. I found her shivering under the passenger's seat, all eyes. She was my only cat who could travel without a carrier, often snugged under my right elbow.*

*She was 14 years old when a virulent type of bone cancer struck her down. I kept her alive for 6 months after the vet's diagnosis. I'd decided to end her life when, for the first time she was incontinent on a pillow. The day before we were to make the final visit to the vet, she died in my arms. I think she wanted to spare me that decision.*

*For months afterwards, I woke up to her paw on my hand. When I cleaned areas she'd been in, I'd hear her sweet little voice. I could feel her brush against my legs. I knew she was still there.*

*About 12 years later I stopped dreaming about her—chasing after her through burning buildings, feeling more like being led through the fire—without her could I find my way? For an even longer time I'd notice her out of the corner of my eye, feel her presence at odd moments throughout the day. In desperate times, I could feel her close.*

*I moved, and she came with me. Her ashes are with me still, but I believe she hovers near, with or without them, her spirit boundless.*

*I have new cats. When she died, I'd vowed never to get another. Losing a cat is too painful. But a kitten needed me, and then another, and, after they passed, three more. They probably need me less than I need them. Melanie has not been a physical presence over the last 8 years—I can't find her when I think of her. Perhaps she knows I need her less, or perhaps she's finally settled peacefully into whatever version of heaven animal companions have. She deserves the peace.*

## A Connected Cat

Our friend Merle's cat, Seamus, passed away on the same day as Stan's [her late husband] birthday. That's not a coincidence. Seamus and Stan are together in the light. Merle shared that after Stan passed, Seamus showed anger if he was left alone. She said Seamus developed quite an "attitude." After Seamus passed, Merle has heard what sounds like kitty footsteps in the house, but said, "It could just be the house creaking." I happen to think that it is Seamus coming back to visit from time to time.

## Horses and Birds

Although horses and birds have a different level of intelligence than dogs and cats, they do understand human language, respond to commands, and exhibit body language and emotion. They also exhibit different types of intelligence as mentioned in Chapter 4, such as instinctual and emotional intelligence, routine, location, vocal and body language, facial signals, and Kinesthetic intelligence (ability to move the body around obstacles).

## Horses: Ghosts and Spirits

I have never encountered the spirit of a horse who was attempting to communicate with someone still living, but if I spent more time on a ranch or a farm, I am certain that I would.

I have, however, witnessed the residual energy of the ghosts of horses, particularly in cities where horses would have been the primary mode of transportation. Examples of where this has occurred include outside of Montpelier Mansion in Laurel, Maryland, and the Josiah Quincy House in Quincy, Massachusetts, where I saw a horse drawn carriage.

At the Montpelier Mansion, I saw images of the residual energy of horse-drawn carriages ghosts. Men, women, and children dressed in period clothing exited the carriages and entered what would have been the front entrance to the mansion at that time.

Similarly, when I visited the historic Josiah Quincy House in Quincy, Massachusetts, on one side of the house I saw vivid images of men, women, and children dressed in colonial period attire, and again saw images of horse-drawn carriages in front of the home.

In her book, *When Ghosts Speak,* Mary Ann Winkowski writes about seeing ghost race horses on a racetrack in Kentucky. She noted that the ghostly horses can be seen by the living horses, and these apparitions are often frightening to them.

In speaking with a friend of mine who has been on the Eastern U.S. rodeo circuit for many years and also a horse owner, I learned a lot about horses and their intelligence and abilities. It is my sense that horses do not have a large understanding of vocabulary, but they do understand human emotions. My friend noted that horses, like dogs, can tell when their rider is stressed, upset, or happy and react to their emotions.

## Horses Can Sense Ghosts and Spirits

As with dogs and cats, horses can sense, see, and hear spirits. Horses can also hear at higher frequencies than humans - the same frequency levels ghosts and spirits are believed to communicate. Humans have to use digital recorders pick up communications from Spirit at higher frequencies.

At one of Barb Mallon's medium sessions a gentleman from Africa told me that in his country (I can't recall which country) tradition says that if a person looks directly in the eyes of a horse, one can see the same ghost or spirit that the horse can see.

An internet search of the words "horses see ghosts" will produce a lot of stories from horse owners where their horses would not enter stalls where another horse has died, or where the ghost of human as seen to enter.

## Bird Communicators

According to PetMD, there are a number of species of birds that can be taught to speak in human language. Birds classified as Amazons are known for having the ability of speech, but the number of them that have that ability are limited.

Some birds that have a limited ability of speech include: Budgerigar, Monk Parakeet, Blue-Fronted Amazon, Indian Ringneck, Eclectus, Yellow-Crowned Amazon, Double Yellow Head Amazon, Hill Myna, Yellow-Naped Amazon, and African Grey.

A number of the birds mentioned here can mimic human language, but the African Grey is thought to have the ability to relate concepts, similar to a human toddler. According to PetMD, the African Grey is considered to be among the smartest of the talking birds.

I have previously shared the story of a parrot owner whose deceased bird has communicated with her through signs. She had her bird for 30 years and she told me that whenever the phone rang, the parrot would imitate the ring. After the parrot passed, she said she would continue to hear what sounded like her parrot imitating the phone's ringing. Apparently, her parrot was giving her a call from the afterlife.

Animals possess the ability to convey messages to the living from Spirit; a species' propensity to comprehend human language facilities can affect this ability.

Based on my experiences dogs and cats seem to have developed this ability more fully than other animal species. But an animal species' inability to develop a vocabulary, or inability to comprehend human language may affect our ability to recognize and understand communications from a pet in the afterlife.

# CHAPTER 14: PETS CAN SENSE GHOSTS AND SPIRITS

Dogs and cats possess the ability to see ghosts and spirits. They are able to do this is because the cones and rods in their eyes differ from humans and enable them to see movement that occurs at higher frequencies.

According to Alexandra Horowitz's book entitled, *Inside of a Dog*, [our pets] can see movement more easily than people can, although they do not see as many colors as people.

Cone cells can detect different colors while rods are for sensing motion and function best in low light. Both cones and rods receive light in the retina.

It is the cones that allow us to see color. Animaleyecare.com says that people and cats have three types of cones, although cats do not have the same vision as humans. Dogs have two types of cones and are red-green colorblind.

I have noted that our Weimaraner and Dachshund are attracted to toys that are yellow and blue in color, much more than to toys of other colors, which may appear to be shades of grey to them.

Horowitz stated that dogs see the world faster than humans do, and see more of the world every second. She said that television does not keep a dog's attention because dogs see the images as individual frames with dark spaces in between, similar to a strobe light. Human eyes, however, do not see the dark screens between the moving images. Ghosts and spirits move at a higher vibrational frequency than the human eye can see, but not so fast that they escape detection by a dog or cat.

In the physical world, a dog's ability to see motion better than humans is what enables them to spot the movements of say, a squirrel that may be a significant distance away, although they may be unable to identify the movement as being generated by a squirrel specifically.

Dogs can only see clearly up to about 75-100 feet away. Because of the genetic makeup of a dogs' eyes, they are less capable of recognizing colors; most colors appear gray, except for yellows and blues.

Like dogs and cats, horses share the same ability to see motion better than humans. Dogs, cats, and horses possess a better visual acuity or the ability to see details than humans. According to Animaleyecare.com, a horse's visual acuity is about 20/33 (a little worse than a human's 20/20 or perfect vision). What's interesting about a horse is that horse's visual acuity is even better than dogs who see at 20/50, and cats who see at 20/75. That means that horses are capable of seeing ghosts or spirits even better than a dog or cat!

Dr. Stanley Coren, DVM wrote in his book, *How Dogs Think,* that dogs hear at higher frequencies than humans, which is very likely that range where ghosts and spirits "talk."

Humans have to rely on digital recording devices to pick up sounds at those higher frequencies. Humans hear up to about 12,000 Hertz, while the highest ranges some dogs can hear ranges as high as 47,000 to 60,000 Hertz. Hertz is the equivalent of cycles of sound waves per second.

Ghost hunters always carry digital recorders with them during investigations and play them back to hear ghostly voices that were not audible to their ears. Those sounds that the recorder picks up are Electronic voice phenomena or EVPs.

## Our Dog on a Ghost Investigation

On November 11, 2013 Inspired Ghost Tracking (IGT) was requested to investigate a private residence in Maryland. The homeowners informed Margaret Ehrlich, manager of IGT, that they believed they were hearing and sensing the spirit of their recently deceased dog. Margaret shared this information with the investigative team, at which time we discussed the enhanced abilities of dogs to see and sense spirits. A request was made to the homeowners to see if they would allow us to bring our Weimaraner, Dolly, along with us to the investigation to see if she would pick up on anything. The homeowners granted permission and the following account is taken from the actual investigation report, although the names of the homeowners have been changed.

**INSPIRED GHOST TRACKING INVESTIGATION REPORT**
**DATE: Nov. 11, 2013**
**TEAM: Margaret, Troy, Tom, Rob, Ronda, and Dolly the Weimaraner**

CINDY THE DOG'S SPIRIT
OUTSIDE: As Tom, Rob, Troy and Dolly were driving into the neighborhood, Dolly awoke from the back seat of the vehicle and

started to get anxious. We pulled past the home and parked, and Dolly was anxious to get out of the vehicle.

Dolly exhibited the same behavior she does when she comes to a familiar area, which didn't make sense because we had never been in this part of the town before.

Rob took Dolly out of the truck and she pulled him down the street, down the driveway of the correct house and right to the front door! Dolly paced around the front door until Margaret walked down the driveway to the front door of the house and knocked on it. It was obvious that Cindy's spirit came to bring Dolly to the house so Dolly would help prove she was still there.

INSIDE: Once inside the house, Dolly seemed disinterested in the first floor for the most part, and went to the stairs leading to the second floor. It was as if the spirit of Cindy came inside, went in the kitchen and looked around and walked back to the main staircase and Dolly was following.

(Margaret of Inspired Ghost Tracking followed Dolly to the front door of the home where the spirit of the dog Cindy lingered. Credit: R. Gutro)

When Rob asked Dolly if she wanted to go up, she pulled him upstairs and made a beeline directly into a little boy's bedroom. It was in that room that Dolly wanted to stay. This made perfect sense to the owners, who said that Cindy always went in their son's room and stayed there. What's interesting is that Cindy didn't often go in their little girl's room, and neither did Dolly. We concluded that the route that Dolly took was the same route that Cindy's spirit took to always check on the boy.

CONCLUSION: Both Rob and Troy sensed Cindy's presence in the upstairs hallway going back and forth between the girl's room and the boy's room, as if looking in to check on them. Her spirit seemed like it went fully into the boy's room, but poked her nose into the girl's room. Cindy is a strong and loyal spirit who feels her job is to watch over the children. When they went downstairs Rob got the sense of running up and downstairs (it turns out it was the stairs leading from the first to the second floor).

SUGGESTION: Getting another dog may alleviate Cindy's responsibility. If Cindy's spirit is keeping anyone awake, talk with her as if she is still alive. Tell her to "go downstairs" or "go to sleep." This is a good spirit, a protective spirit.

## A Dog Sees a Dog's Spirit

Many times people who have dogs or cats that pass find that any new pets they adopt can see or sense their late pets. If you've lost a pet, that pet could be coming back to visit, just as humans do.

In May, 2009, our friend Craig noted that his newly adopted dog, Gracie would often go into the living room and bark at an empty room. Just months before, Craig has said goodbye to his dog Oprah. It was in the living room that Oprah liked to sit, under the picture window.

So, why would Craig's new dog Gracie bark at Oprah's spirit? Well, she likely thought that Oprah was a living, breathing dog. Dogs can't necessarily tell the difference between a living, breathing dog and a spirit dog in some instances.

## Our Dogs Sensed Several Spirits

In my first two books I wrote about our current dogs and their encounters with spirits. Two of our dogs used to come with me to visit our elderly friend Beverlee.

When Beverlee passed, my partner and I attended her memorial service in the apartment building in which she lived, and they asked us to bring our two dogs (at the time).

During the service, Franklin, our Dachshund began shivering and whining as he did when he saw Beverlee's (late) cat "Stitch" whenever we visited. When we left the service, Franklin stopped whining. Our Weimaraner gave a more noticeable sign. The minister had started the ceremony and said, "Let us pray." There was seconds of silence until Dolly let out one very loud and short bark! Dolly was acknowledging that Beverlee was there in the room, and apparently she was with her cat that had passed, at least according to Franklin!

Franklin is very in tune with spirits. When he came with us to Tom's grandmother's cemetery for the first time, he dashed out of the car ran up a hill and sat on her grave. He obviously saw her there!

Another instance when our two dogs sensed a spirit is when our friend Sarah's spirit visited. Sarah loved dogs, had five with her husband and worked for rescues. Shortly after she passed, I sensed Sarah's spirit come into the room. At the same time our dogs all focused on the corner where I sensed her standing.

Finally, one morning in October of 2012 (around the week of my birthday) after my better half went to work, I climbed back in bed and put our three dogs, Dolly, Franklin and Sprite on the bed. As I was lying in bed, I clearly heard my dad's voice call my name from the kitchen! At the same time I heard his voice, all three dogs turned their heads toward the kitchen. They also heard my dad's voice! My dad passed away 4 years before in 2008. This proved that not only do dogs hear spirits, but also that spirits come back around our birthdays, anniversaries or special holidays.

**Recognizing When Your Pet May See a Spirit or Ghost**

So, how do you know when dogs see ghosts and spirits? If a dog reacts as he/she would when an actual person walks into the room, but there is no one there, you may have a ghostly visitor. If you find your dog or cat staring at a corner of the room and there's no one there that you can visibly see, there may be a ghostly or spirit guest.

Professional ghost investigators use digital recording devices to pick up sounds at higher frequencies that cannot be heard by the human ear. It's likely that dogs may even hear spirits when they speak, although humans may not, simply because dogs hear at higher frequencies.

**Ann's Dogs See Her Father Pass Away**

The following story was shared by my friend Ann who believes that her father's service dog, a standard poodle named Cowboy and his sibling, Peaches, saw the spirit of her father leaving his body when he passed away at home.

**(Cowboy watched Ann's dad pass. Credit: Ann McD.)**

Ann wrote: *Peaches and Cowboy were in my Dad's room when he died. He was under hospice care, and they had been hanging out with him all day. Just as he died, they both jumped up, barked once, went to the front door, and then came back. Then they wandered off. They clearly knew he had died and was gone.*

## Bacardi the Dog Sensed Several Spirits

In my first book I shared a story from a man named Jim who said that his dog Bacardi seemed to have an affinity for seeing spirits. In one incident, Bacardi began barking at four 6" by 4"oil paintings on wood painted in 1939 by Carl Roth that belonged to his paternal grandmother. Jim said his dog barked at the paintings until he was told to stop. As Bacardi was barking, Jim said he felt a cold breeze move through him. It was apparently a ghost or spirit that was attached to the painting, likely that of his grandmother checking in.

Later, Bacardi apparently saw the spirit of Jim's mother while Jim and his dog were in the basement. Jim was doing laundry when his dog stood still and stared at Jim's mother's belongings for more than five minutes. Apparently, Jim's mom was visiting while Jim was doing laundry to make sure he was doing it correctly!

## Cats See Spirits

During one of my promotional book events a man told me that his cat would often stare at an area in his basement. He said that one time, a white mist (ectoplasm, apparently) came from the corner and the cat ran. I've spoken to many other cat owners who have shared the same experiences.

## Anne Marie's "Psychic Kitty"

Following is a story from Anne Marie Clarke about her beloved pet, whom she calls a "psychic kitty." Anne Marie wrote:

*My cat, Madison (a.k.a. Madison Gabrielle Clarke) was born around April 1, 2000. She was another cat that I rescued from Long Beach, California.*

*Maddie is sweetness on 4 legs. She hasn't a mean bone in her body. Even when she play-hunts, she's very innocent about it. She has two goals in life. Food and love. She meows A LOT and I believe that in addition to 89 other kinds of cats, she also has some Siamese in here, which explains the meowing. Maddie isn't exactly the brightest bulb in the ol' chandelier. However, Maddie is my psychic kitty.*

*I have often caught her staring at the SAME spot in our apartment. She has two spots, in particular, that she stares at and meows her little head off. They are both corners in the ceiling – one in our living room and one in our bedroom. (I have caught the other cats looking at the ceiling corner in both these spots, as well, but nobody focuses on them like Maddie. I have no idea what she's trying to tell me, or what she sees. But she definitely sees something.*

*I have, on a few occasions, tried to turn her away from looking at the spot she stares at, just to see what she'll do. She comes back to it and stares. It's very cool to watch.*

*As for her intelligence, while she does come across as somewhat dim, she has learned (because we taught her) how to play Hide and Seek. Every night, she'll hop up on our bed and flip flop on it (out of happiness). She then looks at us, and we have to play "the game." We ask her, "Are you ready?" Then we put a sheet over her and say, "Where's Maddie?" And she meows back. We then pet her and say, "There she is!" This can go on for 10 or 15 times, and it is a nightly ritual. Maybe she's as weird as her owners. But she knows how to play that game. When she stops answering the question of "Where's Maddie?" we know that, for her, the game is over.*

## CHAPTER 15: PET SPIRITS ASSIST, WAIT FOR US

While living with my parents, my family had two dogs (as I mentioned in the Introduction). The first dog was a Cocker Spaniel named Penny the Cocker Spaniel and the second was a Miniature Poodle named Gigi. Looking back at how Gigi came to live with us, it is my belief that my parents were guided to her with the help of Penny's spirit. About five years after Penny passed, my mother decided that she wanted the next family dog to be a poodle, so my dad began contacting several local dog breeders to see what was available.

As fate would have it, one of the breeders that my dad contacted had a poodle puppy that had been recently returned with a broken leg. I do not remember the circumstances behind how Gigi's leg came to be broken, but I do recall thinking at the time that it was really cruel for a dog to be returned for such a minor injury.

Although Gigi was labeled as the family dog, she was definitely my mother's dog. I recall many failed attempts at trying to get Gigi to sleep through the night with me in my room, as she would always jump out of the bed and run down the hallway to my parents' bedroom. I also loved Gigi very much, and even drew a series of comic books where the lead dog character was inspired by her. Eventually, I moved away from home to attend college, but I always looked forward to seeing Gigi on my return visits to home.

**(Gigi and Rob in 1979. Credit: R.Gutro)**

In 1993, I was 30 years old and on a work detail in Miami, Florida when I received a call from my parents. I remember sitting in the hotel room at the desk when my mother told me that Gigi had passed. Gigi was 18 years old, very frail, sickly, and in a lot of pain. My parents made the decision. I remember sitting in that hotel room in Miami by myself crying on the phone with my mother.

My parents bought a plot for Gigi's remains in a pet cemetery in Hanover, Massachusetts. They dutifully visited Gigi's plot every month right up to the time of my own mother's passing in December 2013. Like all good pet owners, Gigi was like a child. The pain subsides, but the grieving and sense of loss continues. Our dogs are forever in our hearts.

Gigi provided me with a sign – the first I ever received from her – about 15 years after she passed, and she was not alone.

**Our Family Dogs Waiting for My Dad**

In August 2008, at my dad's graveside services, mourners and family members were gathered under a tent on a very rainy, New England day. It was there that I witnessed several dogs waiting in the light for my dad just before he crossed.

Just as the service was drawing to a close, I saw a bright white light open up on a hillside to the right of where my dad was to be interred. I asked my sister-in-law seated beside me if she could see it. She confessed that she did not. Up until that day, I had never before witnessed the physical manifestation of the light that admits spirits to the other side. It was truly amazing. I looked up on the hill where the light was emanating and I saw figures standing in the light coming into focus. From right to left were my grandmother (my dad's mother) holding an infant (my dad's brother who died at birth), grandma's second husband, her first husband (my dad's father), and then my mom's parents. Sitting in front of them were three dogs: my parent's dogs Penny and Gigi; and my puppy Buzz.

Then I sensed my dad walking past my mom and all of us who were gathered under the tent. I then watched my dad cross into the light. The light faded as the service ended and people turned away to depart. It was truly amazing to witness all three dogs waiting in the light for my dad on the other side.

When it comes our time to pass, our dogs and cats will also be waiting in the light for us.

**Our Family Dogs Waiting for my Mom**

On Sunday afternoon, December 22, 2013, my mother suffered a severe stroke. The prognosis for her recovery was not good, and my partner and I were unsure as to when we should make the drive up to Massachusetts. On Friday evening, before we left, I contacted my good friend and medium, Ruthie Larkin. I asked Ruthie if she was able to sense where my mother was, and what spirits might be around her. Ruthie said that she saw the spirit of my dad in the hospital room standing next to her with an outstretched hand, and encouraging her to cross over. But my mom was refusing to take his hand. She was not yet ready to go.

Ruthie also said that she saw the spirits of two dogs. From Ruthie's description, I was able to identify them as Gigi and Penny. Ruthie said that she also saw my dad pick up Gigi and walk her over to my mom's bedside showing her that Gigi was with him and waiting on the other side.

We drove up the next morning and arrived in the afternoon. As I walked into the hospital room, I immediately sensed the presence of my dad. My partner and I told mom that it was okay to go into the light and said our final goodbyes. My mother quietly passed the very next morning on December 29, 2013.

I know that my mom is at peace, and I know that she is with my dad and her two beloved dogs. This is more evidence substantiating that when it is your time to cross over your beloved pets will also be there in the light waiting patiently for you. Until that time, find comfort in knowing that they visit you from time to time.

# CHAPTER 16:   GHOSTLY PETS IN ENGLAND

---

## Fanny and the Architect

In 2012, my partner and I vacationed in the United Kingdom. On the second day of our trip we visited Sir John Soane's Museum. John Soane was a famous architect in England.

Upon entering the house turned museum, I immediately sensed the presence of a ghost, but it was not human. It didn't take long to learn the ghost's identity as we walked through the museum.

The museum contains an amazing collection of architectural fragments, statues, and original paintings from the Renaissance. The basement is literally a maze of priceless artifacts and antiquities. When Soane wanted two of something, he hired the best artisans to faithfully recreate a copy; when placed side by side, it is virtually impossible to detect the recreation.

Of the four levels of this quirky structure, I found the basement level to be the most unnerving. Items on the basement level include an Egyptian sarcophagus, as well as iron chains and manacles salvaged from a prison. I sensed that these items in particular were associated with people that suffered tremendous pain, so I quickly walked past them.

In addition to being a collector Soane was also an accomplished architect who appreciated light-filled interiors. There are skylights throughout the house that allow light to filter down through the structure, even to the basement level. It was a fascinating place to walk through.

**There's a Ghost Dog in Here**

It was on the first floor of the museum that the ghost's identity was revealed. As I walked through the home I looked out a window to an obelisk in a small courtyard. Inscribed on the monument were the words, "Alas, poor Fanny." I told Tom that monument marked the burial site of a dog, and that the presence I was sensing in the house was that of a dog. Fanny was still there.

When we got to the portrait gallery, I was able to confirm that Fanny was Mrs. Soane's beloved dog's name. One of the portraits in the gallery depicted Fanny, a terrier, sitting in the lap of Mrs. Soane.

Later when I was in the gift shop I happened upon a children's book about Fanny. I asked the sales clerk if she had ever sensed the presence of a dog in the house. She looked at me wide-eyed and said, "Yes." She explained that after the Soanes passed, ownership of the house went through several generations of different owners, and each reported sightings of the ghost of a dog in the house. The owners immediately following the Soanes had a dog whom the clerk said "was always anxious and could never settle down."

The clerk told me that a later owner had two Dachshunds whom were also quite nervous in the house and ultimately had to go live elsewhere. The clerk said that "Fanny" has been seen a number of times, particularly running around in the basement.

After John Soane's Museum we visited Hampton Court Palace and I learned of other ghostly pets. I also learned of British monarch who even granted a special position to a certain breed of dog.

**The Phantom Dog**

According to Hampton Court Palace's book, "Is the Palace Haunted: Palace Phantoms," a ghostly dog has been seen and heard at the King's Staircase in the William and Mary section of the palace.

Queen Victoria banned all dogs from the palace except for lap-dogs, but this ghostly presence is reported to be a mongrel dog. No one has a clue as to whether this dog was a pet or a guard dog, but reports from State Apartment Warders (people that work in that part of the building) and others during the 1990s have indicated that a ghostly dog has been seen and heard.

## A Ghostly Cat

Several tourists to Hampton Court Palace have reported stepping over what appeared to be a white cat. What's interesting is that there is no historical documentation substantiating that cats were ever kept as pets by the royal family in the palace.

## King Charles II – the Dog Lover

Historical accounts document that King Charles II was a dog lover. Under royal decree, King Charles II granted King Charles Cavalier Spaniels (named for him obviously) the ability to go anywhere at their leisure within Parliament buildings. The royal decree was referred to as the 'commons dogging charter.' Of course, he was displeased with Parliament, so this was one way of getting back at them. It was obvious that he had an affinity for dogs since a portrait of him as a child depicts a small dog on his lap that resembles a Charles Cavalier Spaniel.

# CONCLUSION

Energy cannot be destroyed, but it can be changed. After physical lives end, the energy within humans and animals combines with memories, personalities and emotions and become an energy as an Earth-bound ghost or spirit in the light. Our loved ones remain with us whenever we call to them, see a photograph of them or think about them. They can come to us in our dreams (if they've passed into the light). They will be waiting for us when it is our time to pass to welcome us into the next life. It is my experience that love never truly dies, and it even transcends from the afterlife to this life. Just keep an open mind, watch for signs and have faith.

## Mediumship is a Puzzle You Have to Put Together

Sometimes the person to whom a message is intended won't immediately understand the significance of a message. Other times, it may be as clear as a butterfly landing near you.

You could also receive messages for the friend of a friend because Spirit knows how we can connect to each other and will pass messages to the most receptive person.

Don't be discouraged if you don't understand something – you may figure it out in time.

Sometimes it's difficult to understand the messages from spirit, and it's easy to mistake their identity. For example, if you find pennies and think it's your late cat, it could very well be a message from your grandmother, or vice versa. You need to study the clues, check what date it is, and the date on the coin. Those things could hold clues to the spirit's identity.

During one of Barb Mallon's medium events I physically saw the spirit of a well-dressed older African American gentleman sitting next to a woman in Barb's audience. The man's spirit told me that he was connected to the young woman.

I assumed (and I shouldn't have) that because the male spirit looked older than the young woman in the audience, that he was a father or grandfather, so I told her that. She was puzzled. I told her the man's spirit watching over her is a "sharp dresser" and loved wearing hats. He was also very dedicated to his Bible and his faith.

At the time, she told me both her grandfathers died when she was young. She was sure that the spirit was not either of them. She left disappointed and confused, and I was puzzled. The spirit was so adamant that he was connected to her.

One week later, the young woman emailed Barb Mallon and said that after discussing my reading with her father she realized the spirit was her uncle!

She said that her dad broke down into tears when she told him all the signs I provided. She said her father's brother passed away and fit the messages perfectly and told Barb to thank me for providing her dad comfort and assurance that his brother was still around and looking after his niece. The lesson I learned from this is not to assume that a spirit is a certain relative, but either an elder or a contemporary (meaning the same age), or someone younger.

So, message from Spirit are a puzzle we all have to piece together to get the answers.

You can get messages, too. Just before going to bed each night ask your loved ones to come into your dreams and keep pen and paper on your nightstand so you can record them when you wake up. Read all you can, believe in your messages (especially if they don't sound like anything you would know) and practice, practice, practice.

## A Final Note: Honoring Your Pet

If you want to honor the memory of your beloved pet, the best thing you can do is to adopt another who is in desperate need of a home. Contact a rescue and save a helpless animal, and share the love you have for the pet you may have lost with another. Our pets that pass tell me that the best way to honor their memory is to help another.

If your friends want to provide comfort to you during your time of grief, ask them to make a donation to an animal rescue in your pet's name. That's a wonderful name to memorialize your pet, and another way to make your pet's spirit smile from the other side.

To follow along on my latest adventures or share your adventures or questions, visit my blog at:

*http://ghostsandspiritsinsights.blogspot.com/*

# WITH APPRECIATION

---

This book would not have been possible without the assistance, time and personal stories from a number of people and /or their special companions.

My thanks to my husband for editing and improving the book, and spending many nights with our dogs watching television while I worked on the book and made arrangements for appearances, interviews and answered emails. I am honored to include the personal stories from so many wonderful people. My thanks to my friends and amazing mediums and their dogs: Barb Mallon, Ruthie Larkin and Troy Cline. I'm grateful to Shelley Sehnert, Audrey Haar, Anne Marie and Simon Clarke, Rebecca and Jeff Elliott, Margaret Ehrlich and Ronda Dixon of Inspired Ghost Tracking, Kathy Martin, Lisa Woodman, Jill Durfee, Diane Schwartz, Craig Bencie Jr., Fay Fowler Gross, Merle McClure, Yolie Aviles, Lisa "the engineer/medium," Jill Joubert, Layla Sarakalo, Ann McDonald, Jim Klein, Ed Kelley, Terri Gregory, Tony's mom Janice, Barney's mom Andrea, Patches' dad Mark, Millie's dad Doug and mom Sue Ellen, Gregory Berns, Attila Andics, Dr. Stanley Coren, Allison Argo, and Sir John Soane's house museum.

# BIBLIOGRAPHY

---

## CHAPTER 3:

Winkowski, Mary Ann; *When Ghosts Speak*, 2007, Grand Central Publishing, New York

## CHAPTER 4:

Hero Dog Saves Wounded Friend, Sonny Melendrez,
http://www.sonnyradio.com/herodog.html

Burns, Gregory; How Dogs Love Us: A Neuroscientist and His Adopted Dog Decode the Canine Brain; 2013; New Harvest

Coren, Stanley; The Intelligence of Dogs; 2006, Pocket Books, Simon & Schuster, UK.

Coren, Stanley; How Dogs Think, 2004, Free Press a division of Simon and Schuster, N.Y., N.Y.

Wikipedia: Magnetic Resonance Imaging.
http://en.wikipedia.org/wiki/Magnetic_resonance_imaging

Andics, Attila; Gácsi, Márta; Faragó, Tamás; Kis, Anna; Miklósi, Ádám; Voice-Sensitive Regions in the Dog and Human Brain Are

Revealed by Comparative fMRI; Current Biology - 20 February 2014;  Source: http://www.cell.com/current-biology/retrieve/pii/S0960982214001237


Langbrain. Temporal Lobe. 2000.  Retrieved February, 2014. http://www.ruf.rice.edu/~lngbrain/cglidden/temporal.html


Smith; Kosslyn, Cognitive Psychology: Mind and Brain. 2007. New Jersey: Prentice Hall. pp. 21, 194–199, 349.


**CHAPTER 13:**

Coren, Stanley; How Dogs Think, 2004, Free Press a division of Simon and Schuster, N.Y., N.Y.


Horowitz, Alexandra; Inside of a Dog, 2009, Scribner a division of Simon and Schuster, N.Y., N.Y.


Animal Eye Care.com; "About Animal Vision, Visual Acuity," 2005.


PetMd.com:

http://www.petmd.com/bird/top_tens/evr_bd_top10talking_birds#.UmXQoRCE5nk

**CHAPTER 14:**

Craig's 365 Blog: *http://craig365photo.blogspot.com*

**CHAPTER 16:**

John Soane Museum website, www.soane.org

Hampton Court Palace, Is the Palace Haunted? Palace Phantoms,
http://www.hrp.org.uk/Resources/Ghosts%20at%20Hampton%20
Court%20Palace.pdf

# ABOUT THE AUTHOR

Rob is an avid dog lover who, with his partner, volunteers with Dachshund and Weimaraner dog rescues. Together, they've fostered and transported many dogs, assessing the dogs at shelters for the rescues, working with coordinators, vets, and shelters to save the lives of dogs.

Rob considers himself an average guy, who just happens to be able to hear, feel, sense and communicate with Earth-bound ghosts and spirits who have passed on.

When not communicating with the dead, Rob communicates with the living. He's a meteorologist by trade who enjoys talking about weather. He speaks at schools, museums, and social organizations about weather. Rob worked as a radio broadcast meteorologist at the Weather Channel and was heard providing forecasts on more than 40 radio stations across the

U.S. He has almost 20 years of on-air radio broadcasting experience.

Rob enjoys taking ghost walks in various cities and visiting historic houses and sites to see who is still lingering behind and encourages them to move into the light to find peace.

He still reads and collects comic books and has always loved the mysterious heroes. Since he was a boy, one of his favorite superheroes has always been the ghostly avenger created in the 1940s called "The Spectre."

If you would be interested in having Rob speak about how our pets provide messages from the other side, or about ghosts and spirits, please contact him through email or his blog.

If you have questions or stories you'd like to share please feel free to write him at Rgutro@gmail.com, or write on his blog: http://ghostsandspiritsinsights.blogspot.com/
Facebook page:
https://www.facebook.com/ghostsandspirits.insightsfromamedium
or
Twitter: https://twitter.com/GhostMediumBook

CPSIA information can be obtained at www.ICGtesting.com
Printed in the USA
LVOW10s1753191016

509436LV00010B/989/P